XIII. HUSSARS.

SOUTH AFRICAN WAR.

OCTOBER, 1899—OCTOBER, 1902.

The Naval & Military Press Ltd

in association with

The National Army Museum, London

Published jointly by

The Naval & Military Press Ltd
Unit 10 Ridgewood Industrial Park,
Uckfield, East Sussex,
TN22 5QE England

Tel: +44 (0) 1825 749494
Fax: +44 (0) 1825 765701

www.naval-military-press.com
www.military-genealogy.com
www.militarymaproom.com

and

The National Army Museum, London
www.national-army-museum.ac.uk

*In reprinting in facsimile from the original, any imperfections are inevitably reproduced
and the quality may fall short of modern type and cartographic standards.*

XIII. HUSSARS.

On October 10th, 1899, the Reservists were called up, and ordered to rejoin on or before the 17th. Out of the 184 Reservists called up, three failed to report themselves.

On November 9th, 1899, two and a half squadrons of the 13th Hussars left Aldershot in three trains, the first leaving at 7.40 p.m., arriving at Liverpool the following morning, and immediately proceeded to embark on the hired transport No. 61, S.S. "Templemore."

The strength on this ship was:— 22 Officers, 1 Warrant Officer, 502 N.C.O.'s and Men, 42 chargers, 400 troop horses.

The Officers on this ship were:—
　　Col. Blagrove, commanding.
　　Major W. C. Smithson.
　　Major F. J. Murphy.
　　Capt. E. A. Wiggin.
　　Capt. and Adjt. J. H. Tremayne
　　Capt. A. H. M. Taylor.
　　Lieut. F. H. Wise.
　　Lieut. J. F. Church.

13th HUSSARS

Lieut. A. Symons.
Lieut. E. W. Denny.
Lieut. H. J. J. Stern.
Lieut. F. G. Bayley.
Lieut. A. W. B. Spencer.
Lieut. J. T. Wigan.
2nd Lieut. J. D. Lyons.
2nd Lieut. W. Pepys.
Lieut. T. H. S. Marchant.
Lieut. Qr.-Mr. G. Rupert.

Attached.

Lieut. R. N. Smyth, 21st Lancers.
2nd Lieut. F. W. Jarvis, Loyal Suffolk Hussars.
Major F. J. Lambkin, R.A.M.C.
Vety.-Major F. Smith, A.V.D.

The remainder of the regiment left Aldershot on November 10th, and embarked the following day at Liverpool on the hired transport S.S. "Montfort."

The strength of the Regiment on this ship was:—4 Officers, 66 N.C.O.'s and Men, 8 chargers, 52 troop horses.

The Officers on board this ship were:—
Major M. A. Close.
Captain L. S. Battye.
2nd Lieut. E. F. Twist.
Lieut. E. R. Clutterbuck, 4th Hussars (attached).

Captain A. H. R. Ogilvy remained in Aldershot in charge of the Reserve Squadron, and had with him 2nd Lieutenant G. H. Hodgkinson, and Lieut. and Riding-Master R. McWalters. The strength of the Reserve Squadron, after the Regiment left Aldershot was just under 400 N.C.O.'s and Men.

The "Templemore," though not a particularly good ship for horses, proved to be a good sea boat. She left the Mersey on November 12th, and arrived at Las Palmas on the 17th, about 7.30 p.m., leaving again at 11 a.m. the following morning, and arrived at Cape Town about 2.30 p.m. on December 2nd, and anchored close to the "Columbia," with the 10th Hussars on board, who were just going in to disembark. There was much sickness among the horses at first, one or more dying daily up to the 24th November, after which date they all improved, and no more died. However, during this time we lost one charger and 21 troop horses.

The news at Cape Town was meagre and vague. It was reported that Methuen had forced the Modder River, but with heavy loss. However, it was certain that Ladysmith was not relieved, which concerned us more, as we were ordered on to Durban, and left Cape Town about 5 p.m., and arrived off Durban about 8 a.m. on December 5th, and crossed the bar at 3.30 p.m. After leaving Cape Town the Disembarkation Officer received a belated order to disembark the 13th Hussars. Attempts were made from East London to intercept the "Templemore," but as she passed that port at night they were unsuccessful.

On November 10th, 2nd Lieutenants J. R. Lyons and W. Pepys were promoted Lieutenants.

We immediately began disembarking, and the following morning entrained for Mooi River, the first train leaving at 7 a.m.

2nd Lieutenant Marchant was left at Pietermaritzburg to collect the transport.

The last train, which left Durban at 11.25 a.m., arrived at Mooi River about 3 a.m. next morning, by which hour it had only been possible to unload one train. The whole of the 7th December was employed in getting the baggage, etc., up to the camp, which was about a mile from the station. Transport was very limited, but Major G. M. V. Hunt, A.S.C., who left the Regiment in 1886, did everything he could to help us.

On the 7th, Major C. Williams rejoined. He had been sent out to Spain in July by the War Office to buy mules.

On the 10th, the Regiment marched to Willow Grange, about 12 miles. Here 2nd Lieutenant Marchant rejoined with transport.

On the 11th, marched about 7 miles to Estcourt, and

On the 12th, joined Lord Dundonald's Brigade at Frere, which consisted of:—

> The Royal Dragoons.
> 13th Hussars.
> Thorneycroft's Mounted Infantry.
> Bethune's Mounted Infantry.
> Natal Carabiniers.
> Mounted Infantry Coy., K.R.R. ⎫
> Imperial Light Horse.   ⎬ Composite Regiment.
> Natal Police.   ⎭

The irregular corps had no signallers, and we were ordered to find them. However, it is presumed that the signallers gave great satisfaction, as the different corps in question raised every difficulty when the men were applied for to rejoin many months after.

SOUTH AFRICAN WAR.

On the 14th, the Regiment marched at 4 a.m. to Chieveley, and during the afternoon Major Close and the party that had sailed on the "Montfort" joined the Regiment.

The South African Light Horse, commanded by Major the Hon. J. Byng, 10th Hussars, joined the Brigade.

The "Montfort," which had on board, besides the detachment of the Regiment, half 61st Battery, R.F.A., and 100 Sappers, under Lieut. Addison, R.E., passed the "Templemore" in the Mersey about noon on November 12th, and sailed for Queenstown, which passage took about 36 hours. Here the 79th Battery, R.F.A. (Major Armitage and Captain Clanville) embarked, and she proceeded to Gibraltar, arriving on the 19th, and after picking up the 6th Fortress Company, R.E., proceeded to Las Palmas, where she coaled, and then on to Cape Town, arriving on December 5th. Here orders were received to proceed to East London, where she arrived on December 8th, and disembarked the Artillery. On the 10th, she sailed again for Durban, arriving on the 13th. The detachment of the Regiment immediately disembarked, and joined the Regiment at Chieveley on the evening of the 14th.

The "Montfort" was a comfortable ship, and the accommodation for the horses was good; however, during the voyage, 11 horses of the detachment died. Although there were over 300 horses on this ship, there was no veterinary officer.

About 8.30 p.m. on the 14th, tents were struck, and we bivouacked for the night.

Just as the Regiment turned out on the 15th there was a remarkable eclipse of the moon. At 4 a.m., Dundonald's Brigade, with 7th Battery, R.F.A., marched out of camp, and moved off to operate against the enemy's left flank. The Regiment was halted on the high ground facing Hlangwani, and the T.M.I. and S.A.L.H. and Composite Regiment went on dismounted to attack this hill. This was a task quite beyond the number of troops that could be employed at this point; and, after losing heavily, they had to etire. Major Williams' squadron was sent to help this retirement. Lieut. Bayley, who had been sent on with the signallers with the Battery, came under a heavy fire, and No. 3133 Pte. Humphrey was wounded, No. 3767 Pte. Wright, signaller attached to the S.A.L.H. was wounded in the attack on Hlangwami. Things had been going worse on the left, and it became apparent that we should not water our horses in the Tugela, as we had hoped when we turned out. About 3 p.m. we got orders to retire, Major Smithson's squadron being sent to escort the Naval guns out of action. One gun was found deserted by the native drivers, and the oxen had scattered; however, other drivers were found, and the oxen collected, and the gun was safely withdrawn.

During the retirement, we heard that Colonel Long's guns had had to be left on the field, and when we arrived at the level crossing close to Chieveley Station an order was received that we were to go out and cover these guns, as an attempt would be made to bring them in after dark. This order was cancelled almost immediately, and about 5 p.m. the Regiment got back to camp, where it had camped the previous day.

SOUTH AFRICAN WAR.

It was a very hot day, with hardly a breath of wind, and the horses had been without water since the evening before. Lieut.-Colonel Blagrove's horse was hit during the morning.

Extract from Regimental Orders, 16/12/99.

"The S.M.O., Cavalry Brigade, Major Lambkin, has brought to the notice of the Commanding Officer the excellent work done by the Regimental Stretcher Bearers in yesterday's action under very trying circumstances. They performed their duties coolly and energetically, and without their aid, a number of wounded belonging to the other Mounted Corps engaged would have had to remain unattended to for many hours. These remarks apply to the whole of the regimental bearers, but the work done by Private Levey has been brought to notice as deserving particular commendation. The Officer Commanding has great pleasure in communicating the above order to the Regiment."

Names of Regimental Stretcher Bearers:—

No. 4311 Pte. Levey.
No. 2974 Pte. Gallagher.
No. 3187 Pte. Thompson.
No. 3917 Pte. Twyman.
No. 2996 Pte. Carstairs.
No. 3879 Pte. Ellis.
No. 1929 Pte. Meadon.
No. 3934 Pte. Smallwood.

On the following day there was an armistice till midnight.

No. 3743 Pte. Billington got into a deep hole when watering his horse, and was drowned, in spite of the efforts of Lieut. Pepys and several men to save him, nor was his body recovered until the 21st.

The Royals and Second Infantry Brigade marched back to Frere at midnight, 16th—17th; and the 17th the Regiment moved out at 3 a.m., and was out all day watching the front, while the Camp was moved back nearer to Chieveley Station. During the day C Squadron had two horses hit. This was a very hot day, and water for the horses very hard to find.

December 18th and 19th, quiet days.

December 20th, a detached post under Lieut. Denny was surprised on Hussar Hill, and No. 3016 Pte. Ross and No. 4051 Pte Smith were killed.

From December 21st to January 4th, the Regiment was continually employed on outpost duty, and clearing farms, cattle guards, water picquets, etc.

On December 23rd, 2 officers and 20 men of B Squadron were ordered to turn out, and were naturally disgusted when it was known that the sole reason for this turn out was for them to be cinematographed.

Extract from Field Force Orders, 1/1/00:—

"The following message has been received from Sir A. Bigge-Osborne by the G.O.C. in Chief:

"Please communicate following from Queen to all troops in S. Africa, including Ladysmith, Kimberley, and, if possible, Mafeking.

" 'Wish you all a bright and happy new year. God bless you all.' V.R.I."

On January 5th, A and C Squadrons, and all the Irregular Cavalry reconnoitred towards Hlangwani. The guns fired several shots at the hills, and we returned to camp at 4 p.m.

January 6th. The Ladysmith guns could be heard about 2 a.m., and continued on well into the day, At 2 p.m. the whole Division turned out, and demonstrated against the Boer position at Colenso, with the object of bringing the Boers back from Ladysmith. Many Boers could be seen coming down from the hills, and going into the trenches. Our Artillery fired several shots, but the Boer Artillery did not return the fire.

Returned to camp about 7.30 p.m.

The Natal Army Orders of the 8th told us that the Boers had made a most determined attack on Cæsar's Camp and Wagon Hill, which had been gallantly repulsed by Sir George White's troops.

January 7th, 8th, and 9th, quiet days.

Orders were received that when a move was made the Regiment would be disposed as follows:—

- A Squadron, Divisional Cavalry, to General Clery's Division.
- B Squadron, Divisional Cavalry, to General C. Warren's Division
- C and Head Quarters, Corps Troops.

Everybody was delighted at the prospect of an early move. The camp was getting foul, many of the men were beginning to go sick, and most of the officers were beginning to feel seedy, and above all, a move meant, we all thought, the relief of Ladysmith.

On January 10th Lt.-Colonel Blagrove took over command of the troops at Frere; and Major Close assumed command of the Regiment. The night of the 9th was very wet, and when the transport moved the next day, it continually stuck, and, to make matters worse, Clery's and Warren's transport had to use the same road, except for the first few miles. As had been generally predicted, both Divisions were to move towards, Springfield, Warren's Division coming from Frere.

The strength of the Regiment on leaving Chieveley was 26 officers, 1 W.O., 481 N.C.O.'s and men, 400 horses, 52 chargers.

A Squadron marched at 6 a.m., and bivouacked near Pretorius Farm, and were lucky in getting their baggage.

C Squadron, less Lieut. Denny and his troop, who were escorting Sir R. Buller's baggage, marched at 8 a.m. Just before reaching camp two very bad drifts had to be crossed. The party of H.M.S. "Terrible," under Lieut. Ogilvy, R.N., who had got over before the squadron, very kindly gave the men tea and something to eat. The last of the Squadron baggage got into camp about 11 p.m. Many units did not get their transport over the first drift even that night, and it was owing to the exertions of Lieut. Jarvis, who was performing the duties of transport officer, that the squadron got theirs.

B Squadron, who had found the night out-posts, marched about 9 a.m., and did not arrive at their bivouac at Pretorius Farm until about 11 p.m. Their baggage was a long way behind.

SOUTH AFRICAN WAR.

On the 11th, C Squadron and Head Quarters marched to Springfield Bridge, and on the 12th to Springfield Camp, and on the 13th to Spearman's Camp.

On the 11th, B Squadron marched to Springfield Camp, where they stayed till the 16th, chiefly employed in escorting waggons, etc.

A Squadron stayed at Pretorius Farm till the 14th.

On the 12th, they reconnoitred towards Chieveley, and exchanged a few shots with the enemy, who were on the north side of the river, but had no casualties; on the 14th, they marched to Spearman's Camp; on the 16th, the baggage was left at Spearman's Farm Camp, and both divisions marched by night, and bivouacked above Trichaard's Drift.

On the 17th, the R.E. pontooned the river, and about 2.45 p.m. the mounted troops began to cross the drift. The river was much swollen after the recent rains, the current was swift, and the bottom rocky—not a nice place to cross—especially as the drift ran slantways upstream. No. 4049 Pte. Prince, and No. 2862 Pte. Guiler were both swept down stream. Pte. Prince would undoubtedly have been drowned, had not Lieut. F. H. Wise swum out to his assistance. Pte. Guiler, though a good swimmer, was so handicapped by his accoutrements that he was carried away, and, in spite of gallant efforts on the part of Trooper David Sclanders, Natal Carabiniers, to save him, was drowned. Captain Tremayne, who went to Pte. Guiler's assistance, would also have been drowned, had not Trooper Sclander saved him. Trooper Sclanders received the Royal Humane Society's silver medal, and Lieut. Wise and Capt. Tremayne the bronze medal.

After crossing the river C Squadron and Head Quarters bivouacked near Venter's Spruit.

A Squadron crossed the river the following morning, and joined C and Head Quarters.

B Squadron crossed by the pontoon bridge about 10.30 a.m., and stayed with the 5th Division.

Lord Dundonald now had with him
    Two Squadrons Royal Dragoons.
    Two Squadrons 13th Hussars.
    S.A.L.H.
    T.M.I.
    B.M.I.
    Natal Carabineers, 1 Co., K.R.R. Mounted Infantry, 1 Co., I.L.I.

This force went on nearly to Acton Holmes, and it was expected that we would soon be busy with the enemy's right, and hoped that the result would go far to obtain the object of these operations—the relief of Ladysmith. However, on the 20th the Brigade was back again near Venter's Spruit. The A and C Squadrons supported the S.A.L.H., under Child's Hill. Both squadrons came in for a bit of shelling, and were lucky not to have had any casualties. Lord Dundonald commended No. 3376 Corpl. F. Smith, and No. 3355 Pte. Servey for good and gallant work as signallers on Child's Hill. Pte. Servey's flag had seven bullet holes through it. Both these men were mentioned in dispatches. During the morning of the 19th, Lieut. Symons with his troop (B Squadron) reconnoitred towards the Boer position, obtaining useful information, for which he was commended by Sir C. Warren.

On the 19th, B Squadron formed an escort to guns on the hill about one and a half miles N.E. of the drift. About 2 p.m. the Squadron moved along the ridge opposite the Boer position, and soon drew their fire. The Boers were on a kopje about 800 yards off, and the Squadron came under a heavy fire. Lieut. Smythe's troop was obliged to retire. No. 3654 Corpl. Coghlan, and No. 4126 Pte. Findlay were both severely wounded. The squadron was reinforced by some infantry, and at 5.30 p.m. retired to their bivouac.

On the morning of the 21st C and A Squadrons returned to the bivouac on Venter's Spruit that they had occupied on the 18th. They formed outposts, etc., on the left flank.

B Squadron had a horse hit on the 21st, but their duties had principally been cattle guards, etc.

Lieut. Spencer went to Hospital, and was invalided home. He rejoined the Regiment at Newcastle, Natal, on October 3rd, 1900.

During this time the fighting had been very severe, and the casualties on our side heavy. It was an irritating time for the Regiment, as the news was vague and generally contradictory, and all wanted to do something more active than sit still on the Venter's Spruit bivouac. When, during the morning of the 24th it was officially announced that Spion Kop had been occupied, it was hoped that the Regiment would soon get a chance. From where we were, it could be seen that our troops on Spion Kop were being fearfully shelled all during the day, but with what effect we did not know, and when, on the morning of the 25th, we heard that they had been obliged to evacuate the hill during the night, even the most sanguine must have been depressed.

Shortly after 6 p.m. the next day, in heavy, cold rain, C Squadron moved off to retire, and crossed the river by the pontoon bridge about 11.30 p.m., halting on the south side till about 3.30 a.m., when they moved on to the ground above Trichaard's Drift, where they had halted on the 16th. A Squadron was detailed for rear guard for the whole force, by whose order it is not clear. It is not apparent that a squadron of cavalry was the best available force for this duty, on a very dark and wet night, in a country intersected with barbed wire. General Hildyard remarked what a difficult and nasty task the squadron had to perform. A Squadron crossed the Tugela about 6 a.m., on the 27th, being the last troops over, and joined C Squadron, above Trichaard's drift, and both squadrons returned to Spearman's Camp. During the retirement the Boers opened a very heavy fire all along the line of their position. Presumably they thought that our movements meant a night attack.

B Squadron turned out about 5 p.m., and were employed in marking the line of retirement from Three Tree Hill to Trichaard's Drift. Single men at intervals of 100 yards were posted along this line to keep the troops on the right road. About 4 a.m. they crossed the river, after a very dreary and uncomfortable night, and bivouacked about one and a half miles on the other side, and later on in the day marched to near the Springfield Camp, getting their baggage on the morning of the 28th.

On the 25th, No. 2998 Pte. Judge, who was attached

to General Clery's staff, lost his way, and was taken prisoner, after being severely wounded, and was taken to Pretoria, where he was found when the British troops entered. He was invalided home, and discharged medically unfit from the effects of his wounds.

On the 29th, Major Murphy went to hospital. He was subsequently invalided home, and did not come out to South Africa again.

On the 30th the Brigade reconnoitred towards Hunger's Poort. Turned out at 10 a.m., and returned about 6 p.m. During the day, B Squadron, less Lieut. Smythe's troop, which stayed with Sir C. Warren, marched in and joined the Regiment.

The strength of the Regiment in camp being:—

23 Officers, 1 W.O., 440 N.C.O.'s and Men, and 385 horses.

The strength of the Regiment in South Africa was:—

1 W. Officer, 562 N.C.O.'s and men, 475 horses.

The Regiment remained in camp at Spearman's Camp till February 5th.

On the 1st February, Captain Taylor and Lieut. Bayley joined Colonel Burn-Murdoch's staff, the former as Staff Officer for B duties, the latter as Signalling Officer.

Both these officers remained on General Burn-Murdoch's staff till the cessation of hostilities.

Captain Taylor's dates of appointments being as follows:—

S.O. "B" duties 1/2/00 to 5/6/00.

S.O. "B" duties and A.P.M. 1st Cavalry Brigade, 6/6/00 to 29/8/00.

Brigade Major, 1st Cavalry Brigade (N.A.O. 18/10/00) 30/8/00 to 2/9/00.

A.P.M. 1st Cavalry Brigade (L. of C. Orders 2/9/00).

Brigade Major 1st Cavalry Brigade (A.O.S.A. 30/10/00) 20/10/00.

Graded D.A.A.G. (A.O.S.A. 31/12/00).

Lieut. Bayley in the London Gazette (11/12/00) was graded as a Staff Captain while Brigade Signalling Officer, dated 1/2/00.

On the 2nd February, Lt.-Colonel Blagrove rejoined the Regiment, from commanding the troops at Frere, and the 13th Hussars, Royal Dragoons, and 14th Hussars formed a Brigade under Colonel Burn-Murdoch.

About 6.30 a.m., on February 5th, the Brigade marched in rear of the Infantry, down the hill under Brackfontein, the baggage following after us. We understood that there would be a lot of heavy fighting before our chance came, but that when the Artillery and Infantry had done their work the Brigade would go on, and the relief of Ladysmith would be a matter of history. The Regiment was practically dismounted all the day under Swartzkop, from where we had a good view of the feint on our left, which began the battle of Vaalkrantz. Five batteries of Artillery were pushed to the front, and it was a truly grand sight to see the gunners serving their guns under a heavy shell fire, and when the object of the feint attack had been obtained, retiring with the same orderly pre-

SOUTH AFRICAN WAR.

cision that we have so often seen on the Long Valley. Then we saw the Infantry advance across the river, and when we bivouacked at night, it was generally thought that decided progress had been made.

Dawn the next morning, February 6th, was somewhat hazy, but it soon cleared off, and about 5.30 a.m. the big gun from Dornkloof sent a shell unpleasantly close to our bivouac. While the horses were being led away, two or three more shells came pretty close, and the last one burst in the middle of A Squadron. Luckily not a single man or horse was hit. This gun afforded our big guns plenty of occupation, but was never knocked out, though it is said that a magazine close to it was blown up by one of our shells.

We did nothing all day, but wished we knew more of what was going on. We bivouacked that night further back towards Potgeiter's Drift.

The next day we moved still further back, and put the lines down. About 6.15 p.m. an order was received to saddle up at once, and about 7 p.m. we marched back to Spearman's Camp, arriving about 9 p.m. with the certain knowledge that this, the third, attempt to relieve Ladysmith had failed.

Vety.-Major F. Smith, A.V.D., left us here to proceed to the Cape Colony for duty, and Vety. Lieut. Houston, A.V.D., was attached to us.

The management of the transport during these operations, was a matter of difficulty. The road down to the plain from Spearman's was very steep, and the road under the hill was in many places very narrow, so that blocks were frequent, and it was really a good performance getting the wagons back in the time it was done. Lieut. F. Jarvis, who was in charge of the Brigade transport, always got his wagons up, and Colonel Burn-Murdoch particularly commended him for the way in which he performed his duties at this time.

On February 10th, the tents were struck at 9 a.m., and wagons packed, and sent on to Springfield, A and C formed an outpost line to cover the retirement of the baggage, and B in reserve. We left Spearman's Camp about 6.90 p.m., and arrived at the camp above Springfield Bridge about 10 p.m., and found the tents pitched and a meal ready.

The Brigade formed a part of a detached force, consisting of the Royal Dragoons, 13th Hussars, 14th Hussars, two Naval guns, and the York and Lancaster Regiment, and the I.L.I., the whole under Colonel Burn-Murdoch.

We stayed at Springfield Camp till February 21st. During this time the duties consisted of patrolling and outposts chiefly.

On the 12th, a Squadron of the Royals on outpost duty was surprised, and had an officer and five men wounded, and an officer and seven men captured. C Squadron, inlying picquet, turned out, and were out all day. The Boers put three shells quite close to them during the afternoon from Dornkloof, a range of six and a half miles.

On the 14th and 15th, the enemy was reported in considerable numbers in the vicinity, but did not put in an appearance.

On February 17th, we heard that General French had relieved Kimberley.

On the 19th, a large box of chocolates came for the men from Mrs. Wise, a gift that was much appreciated.

On February 21st, the Brigade moved to Chieveley, and the next day bivouacked under Hlangwani.

On the 23rd, we crossed the Tugela by the pontoon bridge, under shell fire from Pieter's, which continued all day, and bivouacked under Fort Wylie, a dirty place after three months' occupation by the Boers. Here the Boers had left behind a large quantity of ammunition of every description soft-nosed and hollow-nosed included.

On the 24th, about 2 p.m., B Squadron, still less Smythe's troop, went out to escort the R.H.A., and stayed with them on and near Monte Christo until February 28th, when they rejoined. About 4 p.m. the Brigade recrossed the Tugela by the drift near the Bridge, and bivouacked south of Colenso.

On the 25th, the Brigade moved to the hill north west of Hussar Hill, and C Squadron went on to Weenan.

On the 26th, the Brigade moved back to Colenso, and as soon as we got the lines down, we were ordered to saddle up, and marched back to Chieveley in a drenching rain. C Squadron rejoined from Weenan late in the evening, leaving Lieut. Wise and 21 men there.

On the 27th, the Brigade left Chieveley at 10 a.m., and marched again to Hlangwani, and witnessed the attack on, and taking of, Pieter's Hill. This day we heard that Cronje and his army had been captured.

On the 28th, we crossed the river again, for the fifth and last time. About 4 p.m., the mounted troops were pushed on, and A Squadron, supported by C Squadron, demonstrated against Umbulwana, coming under shell and Pom-Pom fire, but suffered no casualties. The effect of this demonstration allowed Lord Dundonald and a handful of Irregulars to work round and get into Ladysmith without opposition. At Pieter's Station we found a lot of bread, which the Boers had left behind—a great find, and a pleasant change from hard-tack.

B Squadron rejoined the Regiment.

On March 1st, the Brigade reconnoitred towards Ladysmith. Shortly after starting we met the "Times" correspondent, who had been shut up in Ladysmith. He told us that the Boers had evacuated all their positions. It was hoped, and expected, that we should now push on, and inflict a heavy blow on their hurriedly retreating forces. When we got to the foot of Umbulwana, some Kaffirs told us that the Boer wagons, and even guns were hopelessly stuck some seven or eight miles further on. Lt.-Col. Blagrove received a peremptory order from the Brigadier that he was not to go on, and this was repeated in writing a few minutes later. After this we filed along the road round Umbulwana —for what purpose it is hard to conceive, unless it was to show us the peculiarities of the Boer equipment. White satin shoes, and several articles of clothing that no male Boer ever wore, were found. When the head of the column got in sight of Ladysmith, the Brigade turned about, and returned to Nelthorpe. Major Williams and his squadron on the left got into Ladysmith without opposition—the Boers having left their laagers in much haste. Major Williams was asked by Sir George White to take his squadron (A Squadron) on, in support of his troops, till the rest of the cavalry came on. He went out to support General Knox, but a message from Sir R. Buller recalled him, and he returned to Nelthorpe in the evening.

During the Pieter's Hill operations, the cavalry seemed to receive no definite orders, and were continually moved about in what appeared to be an aimless manner.

The G.O.C. received the following telegram from Her Most Gracious Majesty the Queen:—

"To Sir Redvers Buller, Natal.

"Thank God for news you have telegraphed to me. Congratulate you, and all under you, with all my heart. V.R.I."

Sir Redvers Buller issued the following Special Army Order on March 3rd.

"Soldiers of Natal.

"The relief of Ladysmith unites two forces, both of which have, during the last few months, striven with conspicuous gallantry and splendid determination, to maintain the honour of their Queen and Country.

"The Garrison of Ladysmith have, during four months, held their position against every attack with complete success, and endured many privations with admirable fortitude. The relieving force has had to force its way through an unknown country, across an unfordable river, and almost inaccessible heights, in the face of a fully-prepared, well-armed, and tenacious enemy.

"By the exhibition of the truest courage, the courage that burns steadily, as well as flashes brilliantly, it has accomplished its object, and added a glorious page to the history of the British Empire.

"Ladysmith has been held, and has been relieved. Sailors and soldiers, Colonials and home-bred have done this, united by one desire, inspired by one patriotism.

"The General Commanding congratulates both forces upon the martial qualities they have shown. He thanks them for their determined efforts, and he desires to offer his sincere sympathy to the relatives and friends of those good soldiers and gallant comrades who have fallen in the fight."

Up to the end of February the health of the Regiment was exceptionally good. The number of men sick in hospital on the last day of February being 36.

The horses had had no time to acclimatise, and had to be worked straight away, after being on board ship for 24 days. The casualties in horses from all causes up to this date was 108, but it must be understood that many of these were remounts that could not stand the work, and had to be returned to a sick horse depot at the first opportunity.

On March 2nd, the Brigade remained at Nelthorpe. Captain Tremayne went to hospital with enteric, and Lieut. E. W. Denny performed the duties of adjutant till June 24th.

On the 3rd, the relieving force entered Ladysmith, the 2nd Division leading, with the Cavalry Brigade in rear, followed by the 5th Division.

Sir G. White with his staff stood opposite the town hall, and Sir R. Buller at the end of the town. Throughout the day it was a scene of extraordinary enthusiasm.

The Brigade took over quarters in "Tin Town," and were just getting the horses in, when the Boers were reported about five miles off, and the whole Brigade was turned out. Nothing came of this, and in the evening the Brigade returned to "Tin Town."

On the 4th, Lieut.-Colonel Blagrove went to hospital with enteric, and Major Close commanded the regiment till April 21st.

The Brigade remained in Ladysmith till the 6th, when it marched to Elandslaagte, and bivouacked there.

On the 6th, the 5th Dragoon Guards, who had been through the seige, joined the Brigade, but stayed at Ladysmith; and on the 7th the 14th Hussars left for Capetown.

Lieut. Marchant remained in Ladysmith in charge of details.

Lieut. Pepys, who was sick, remained in Ladysmith,

and after a few days went down to Durban; rejoining on the 21st.

On the 7th, A Squadron was sent on to Sunday's River, to form a line of outposts. Lieut. J. T. Wigan was sent on with five men as an officer's patrol, to reconnoitre towards Meran, about five miles distant. After proceeding about three miles, a party of about 30 Boers concealed in a krall opened fire on this patrol. No. 3939 Lance-Corpl. Watt was killed, and Lieut. Wigan and No. 3632 Pte. Rugg were severely wounded. The former in the shoulder, and the latter in the thigh. No. 3897 Pte. Farrance very pluckily came back to Lieut. Wigan's assistance, for which act his name was mentioned in dispatches. Lieut. Wigan was invalided home from the effects of this wound, and rejoined the regiment again in April, 1901.

On the 9th March, moved on to near Sunday's River. On arriving, information was received that the Royals on outpost duty were being attacked, and A Squadron was sent on to support them.

On March 23rd, a draft of 23 N.C.O.s and men arrived

On March 25th, 2nd Lieut. G. H. Hodgkinson joined from England.

In Sir R. Buller's despatch of March 30th, 1900, the names of the following officers, non-commissioned officers and men were mentioned: Lieut.-Colonel H. J. Blagrove, Majors W. Smithson, C. Williams, Captains J. H. Tremayne (adjutant), A. H. Taylor, R. Smythe (attached), Corpl. F. Smith, Ptes. E. Servey, A. Cook.

SOUTH AFRICAN WAR.

On April 5th, No. 3214 Pte. Morris, and No. 3683 Pte. Hazel, were taken prisoners whilst on outpost duty at Weazel's Nek. Pte. Hazel was taken on to Pretoria, and remained there till the occupation by the British troops, and rejoined in November, 1900. Pte. Morris, who was wounded in the leg, was taken on an ox wagon to Newcastle, where Mrs. Potter, the missionary's wife, attended to him. He died from the effects of this wound on May 14th.

The Regiment remained in this camp till April 8th, one squadron being on outpost duty every day.

On April 8th, the Regiment and the Royals left Sunday's River Camp for Star Hill Camp, Ladysmith.

On the 9th, Captain Battye went back to Elandslaagte to take over Capt. Smythe's troops with Clery's division, Captain Smythe having gone sick. C Squadron went as outpost squadron to Thabanyama.

On the 10th, heavy firing was heard in the direction of Elandslaagte. A Squadron with the Royals turned out about 8 a.m. in support.

The Irregulars under Lord Dundonald had taken up the outpost line on Sunday's River, on the departure of the 1st Cavalry Brigade on the 8th. The Boers, finding them not so watchful, attacked them and drove them into camp, which they shelled heavily. The 13th and Royals had held this line for just over a month, and not only obtained good information, but had warded off all attacks.

On the 11th, the camp was moved from Star Hill to Niblick Hill, about one and a half miles.

From this time till the Regiment left Ladysmith on August 4th, one squadron was employed as an advance squadron. This duty was taken in turns by the squadrons, being relieved weekly. At first the advanced squadron was posted at Clydesdale Farm, but on May 25th its position was withdrawn to Arcadia, a nice camp about seven miles from Ladysmith.

On the 23rd, Lieut. Stern's troop was ordered to Blaawbank, as an advanced post, but when the squadron was withdrawn to Arcadia, it rejoined.

Several unburied bodies were found on and near Spion Kop when we first got to Clydesdale.

On the 13th, a draft of 35 N.C.O.'s and men arrived.

On April 17th, and the next few days, Boers were reported to be in the vicinity of Clydesdale, but they did not come on.

On the 20th, 450 of the Queen's chocolate boxes arrived, and were distributed.

On April 21st, Lieut.Colonel Blagrove rejoined from sick leave, and took over command.

On the 25th, Captain Smythe was appointed Signaling Officer 1st Cavalry Brigade.

On the 30th, Major Smithson went down to Durban, sick, and rejoined the Regiment on May 21st.

During the time the Regiment was at Sunday's River, Elandslaagte, and Ladysmith, there was much sickness. During the month of March there were five deaths, and during April there were seven deaths.

SOUTH AFRICAN WAR.

During the months of March and April 106 horses were received from the Remount Department. 35 horses had died, or had been destroyed, and 112 had been sent to the sick horse depot. Horse sickness had been very prevalent during these two months.

The Regiment stayed at Ladysmith during the months of May, June, and July. It was not a healthy place, and very few incidents occurred to relieve the dull monotony. We had a good opportunity of seeing the Boer's positions at Spion Kop and Vaal Kranz, and they were undoubtedly of immense strength.

We also saw the dispositions of Sir George White's troops, and are second to none in our admiration of their gallant defence of Ladysmith.

On the 5th, a draft of 27 N.C.O.'s and men arrived.

On May 7th, B Squadron, under Capt. Wiggin, marched from Ladysmith to Modder Spruit, to act as divisional cavalry to General Clery.

B Squadron was from this date detached from the Regiment, and a record of their services is given separately, and will be found at the end of March, 1901.

During May, Major Lambkin, R.A.M.C., left us, and Captain McLaughlin, R.A.M.C., joined us.

On May 23rd, the Royals and 5th Dragoon Guards, under Gen. Burn-Murdoch, left Ladysmith to be employed in the Ingagane District. The 13th Hussars stayed at Ladysmith, and became part of the Drakenburg Defence Force, under Major-General Downing.

In May, a large consignment of underclothing and

comforts for the N.C.O.'s and men was received. Lady Russell had very kindly interested herself in collecting these articles, and people all over the country had been good enough to assist her. Lady Wiggin also very kindly sent a large package of most acceptable comforts.

On May 17th and 18th, Mafeking was relieved, and on receipt of the news the Regiment sent a wire to Major-General Baden-Powell, congratulating him on his brilliant achievements, and the following reply was received:—

> "Most heartily grateful, warm greetings from the old regiment, and hope we may soon meet at Pretoria. McLaren progressing well."

In July, 1899, Captain McLaren, who was A.D.C. to General Sir Baker Russell, K.C.B., was ordered on special service to South Africa, as Colonel R. S. S. Baden-Powell had applied for his services, and sailed with Colonel H. Plumer and several other officers, arriving at Cape Town on August 2nd. He was then ordered to Bulawayo, and raised the C Squadron of the Rhodesian Regiment. When the war broke out his squadron was at Tuli, near the junction of the Sharki and Limpopo Rivers.

In January, 1900, the column under Colonel Plumer proceeded to Gaberones, and several actions were fought with the Boers, who had a strong natural position near Crocodile Pools. When the Boers retreated south in February, 1900, the Rhodesian Regiment followed them, and worked down to Lobatsi, about 40 miles north of Mafeking, in hopes of relieving the pressure on Colonel Baden-Powell.

On March 31st, Colonel Plumer ordered a demonstration to be made on the Boers near Mafeking by the mounted troops, and in this action Captain McLaren was wounded in three places, and left out for the night on the veldt. The next day he was taken by the Boers to a laager two miles east of Mafeking. He remained there for nearly two months in hospital, and on May 17th, 1900, he was taken to Mafeking, and invalided home in June, 1900.

After several medical boards he was found medically unfit for further service, on accounts of wounds received during the South African War.

The month of June was uneventful. On the 21st, 2nd Lieuts. Gubbins and Lambert, and a draft of 70 men arrived.

On the 29th a Kaffir scout reported to Major Williams at Arcadia that he had heard the Boers announce their intention of taking Mr. Giles, the magistrate of the Upper Tugela, prisoner that day.

Major Williams was ordered to send out a troop to reconnoitre the country between Maria's Hovel and Potgeiter's Drift. One troop was sent out from Niblick Hill, under Lieut. Clutterbuck, to reinforce Arcadia, if necessary. No Boers were seen, and this troop returned to Niblick Hill about 8.15 p.m.

2nd Lieut. Marchant went down to Durban sick on the 26th, and was seven weeks on board the hospital ship "Trojan." After that he was employed on the Remount Department at Durban, till he rejoined the Regiment at Newcastle in October.

At the end of June the number of men sick was very large, viz., 126, nearly all the cases being either enteric or dysentry.

On July 1st, Lieut.-Colonel H. J. Blagrove was promoted Brevet-Colonel. On July 1st Lieut. and Qr.-Mr. G. Rupert, who had been sick in hospital in "Tin Town" for some days, went down to Princess Christian hospital at Pine Town, and was subsequently invalided home. He rejoined the Regiment at Heidelburg on May 2nd, 1902.

Early in the morning of the 7th orders were received to send out a troop to escort rations to meet about 700 Yeomanry and Militia prisoners whom De Wet had released.

Lieut. Jarvis, with a troop, was detailed for this duty, and on the 8th returned to Ladysmith. Most of these prisoners had been captured at Lindley; and, taken as a whole, spoke well of their treatment by the Boers. 78 released Yeomen were attached to us till the end of the month; during which time endeavours were made to instruct the majority of them how to ride the quietest of the worn out horses that were issued to them from the Remount Department in comparative safety.

On the 9th, 2nd Lieuts. Jenkins and Cosens joined from England.

On the 27th, C Squadron moved to Besters. A Squadron stayed at Arcadia. Head Quarters and the men really belonging to B Squadron, with General Clery, to Smith's crossing. These men of B Squadron

SOUTH AFRICAN WAR. 31

had been collected by men coming out of Hospital, and the proportion due to them from drafts.

On the 28th one troop of C Squadron, under Lieut. Clutterbuck, was sent from Besters to Kirkintulloch.

At the end of the month the strength of the Regiment was

With the Regiment near Ladysmith:—
18 Officers, 379 N.C.O.'s and men, 388 horses.

With 2nd Division:—
5 Officers, 99 N.C.O.'s and men, 103 horses.

The health of the Regiment showed little, if any, improvement. There were 81 N.C.O.'s and men in Hospital, and 58 had been invalided home during the month.

On the 28th, the Yeomen attached to the Regiment marched to Modder Spruit, under Lieuts. Stern and Jarvis, and proceeded to Pretoria. Lieuts. Stern and Jarvis rejoined the Regiment at Newcastle on August 21st.

On August 4th, orders were issued in the afternoon for the Regiment to march and occupy Van Reenan's Pass in the night. Everybody was delighted when this order was received. Ladysmith and its immediate vicinity was terribly unhealthy, and the monotony of the life there was hardly ever broken by an incident worthy of note.

Major Spurrell's squadron of the 5th Lancers came with us, and the pass was occupied at mid-night, without opposition. It was bitterly cold on the berg. At dawn the Cavalry moved to Mr. Smith's farm at Albertina, and halted.

The Gloucesters, Derby Militia, and two guns Field Artillery, and a mountain battery of Artillery occupied the pass, and formed posts on the berg.

C Squadron and the Squadron of the 5th Lancers, after a couple of hours halt, went on to Harrismith, where they found General Hector Macdonald had just marched in. They bivouacked that night in the show yard.

At 4.30 the next morning, Major Smithson and C Squadron marched out to Wilge River Bridge—about 6 miles distant—to take over a heavy gun from Gen. Macdonald's force, and to guard it until the arrival of General Rundle's force. After handing over the gun, C Squadron returned to Harrismith, getting in about 10 a.m.

It must be understood that Major Smithson had to start in the dark, without a guide or map, to go six miles in a country he did not know. A guide and a map was applied for, but neither could be supplied.

The next day, August 7th, C Squadron and the Squadron of the 5th Lancers returned to Albertina, where the Regiment remained till the 11th. During this time patrols were sent out over a large area of country to collect arms, but only a few were brought in.

On the 12th, the Regiment marched from Albertina, to Van Reenans.

On the 13th, the Regiment left in six trains for

Newcastle. The first train leaving at 8.30 a.m., and the last train at 9.45. We got into camp about 6 p.m. Half of C Squadron, under Lieut. Wise, went on that night to Donga Spruit; and the next morning Major Smithson took the other half-squadron out to Mathew's Farm.

The strength of the Regiment at Newcastle was:—
16 Officers, 314 N.C.O.s and Men, 140 horses.

With the 2nd Division:—
6 Officers, 142 N.C.O.s and Men, 140 horses.

The half-squadron at Donga Spruit, which had the Maxim with it, were ordered to patrol to Doornkop, and also to patrol to Coetze's Drift, where the 5th Dragoon Guards had a post.

The half squadron at Mathew's Farm were ordered to patrol to Wool's Drift, and also the Nkandu River, and there communicate with the Royals from Duck Pond Farm.

We were told that there was a Boer laager, strength unknown, behind the hills north east of Wool's Drift, and that the main body was at Welgevonden, about 11 miles north east of Wool's Drift.

Patrols were sent out daily from camp in the direction of Muller's Pass, Monkey, and Donkey Passes, and a third to Donavon.

About 6.30 a.m. on the 15th, Lieut. Wise at Donga Spruit received a verbal message from O.C. 5th Dragoon Guards at Coetze's Drift, telling him to bring all his available force to support his right flank, as he was going to attack Dornkop. A party of the 5th

Dragoon Guards had, during the night, stampeded the horses. He got in touch with the 5th Dragoon Guards, but they had been driven back, after having chased a party of Boers beyond Doornkop He then got orders to retire.

The 16th, 17th, 18th, 19th, we did not come in contact with the Boers.

On the 18th, a patrol of the 5th Dragoon Guards from Coetze's Drift were fired on, and the intelligence indicatted that the Boers to the east of Newcastle were in fairly large numbers.

On the 19th, twelve horses were received from the Remount Depot. Five of these were so utterly unsuitable in every way, that after a fair trial they were returned to the Remount Depot. This batch of remounts was possibly worse than the others we received about this time, but not much; and the fact is only mentioned to show that our men, mounted on such worthless brutes were at a distinct disadvantage when patrolling in a country where the enemy was known to be in considerable numbers.

On the 20th, Major Smithson sent in a message to the effect that the troop of the Royals at Duck Pond Farm had been attacked, and had been obliged to retire on Fort Macready. The strength of the Boers was estimated at over 400. Major Smithson endeavoured to cut off the Boers, and proceded to the junction of the Ingagane and Buffalo Rivers, but the Boers retired, and he took his troops towards Wool's Drift.

The squadron turned out from camp, and reconnoitred towards the Ingagane and Buffalo Rivers, but saw no sign of the enemy.

A patrol from Donga Spruit was kept busy this morning. About 250 to 300 Boers were on the flats under Doornkop. A patrol, under Sergt. Miller, was watching them, and the enemy tried to cut them off; however, they recrossed the river safely, and when Lieut. Wise turned out with his inlying picquet, the Boers retired. Pte. Graham's horse fell just as he got to the river, but he hid in some long grass, and though the Boers searched for him they failed to find him, and when Lieut. Wise came out he rejoined him on foot. Lieut. Wise reported that this patrol behaved well, and that No. 3137 Sergt. Miller showed coolness and discretion. All the 5th Dragoon Guards patrols were fired on, and they had two men wounded, and one man taken prisoner.

On the 21st, about 8.30 a.m., information was received that Donga Spruit was being attacked. The squadrons turned out, and went in the direction of this post, but information was received that the enemy had retired. The Boers for some time kept up a very heavy and accurate pom-pom fire on this post, but the horses were well concealed in a donga, and the men well placed under cover, and the only damage done was two mules killed, and a wagon slightly damaged.

Two R.F.A. guns, under Captain Spencer, R.A., and two companies of the Middlesex Regiment were now (11.30 a.m.) on the ridge west of the railway, under Windsor Castle. The two squadrons were ordered to reconnoitre down to the Buffalo River. As soon as the advanced scouts had crossed the river the enemy came on in considerable force, and both squadrons came under pom-pom and rifle fire, and retired to the ridge between two and three miles west of Wool's Drift; when the enemy retired towards Doornkop.

During the day, No. 4624 Private Gilchrist, and No. 4834 Private Willis were slightly wounded, and five horses were wounded.

It had been arranged for Major Smithson's Squadron at Mathew's Farm to be relieved by Major Williams' Squadron, on the 22nd. About 8 a.m. it was reported to Major Smithson that about 200 Boers were crossing the Buffalo River near Wool's Drift. The number of men employed on patrolling duty reduced his half-squadron to a weak troop, with which he advanced to a slight rise (since known as Smithson's Ridge), about one and a half miles west of Wool's Drift, in order to check the Boers' advance, and sent back to Major Williams, who had started, but did not know that the Boers were attacking, to inform him of the situation. This troop (Lieut. Lyon's) was attacked heavily on three sides, and just as Major Smithson gave the order to fall back on A Squadron he was shot through both knees, and No. 3831 Corporal Cooke was wounded in the arm.

The Boer Commandant (Commandant Oppermann) behaved very courteously to Major Smithson. He sent in one of our men whose horse had been shot, and who had been taken prisoner, to get an ambulance, and to conduct it to Major Smithson.

The effect of Major Smithson's fine resistance against

overwhelming numbers, was that A Squadron had time to come out, and engage the enemy well away from the town, and it also gave the guns time to be brought out, and though C and A Squadrons frustrated the attack, a round or two caused the Boers to retire, and they were eventually driven back across the Buffalo River.

No. 4020 Private Dempsey, A Squadron, dismounted from his own horse on seeing a comrade whose horse had been shot, and assisted him on to his own horse, and was shot when retiring, holding on to the stirrup. This gallant soldier died within an hour, but had he lived his name would have been brought forward for a V.C.

Lieut. Jenkins was taken prisoner, and the effort of No. 3931 Private Herbert to bring him in calls for special mention.

Lieut. Jenkins' troop dismounted to cover the retirement of the troop of C Squadron, and when Major Williams gave the order for this troop to mount to take up another position, Lieut. Jenkins' horse, while being brought up to him by Private Herbert, fell apparently shot. Private Herbert rode on to Lieut. Jenkins, and offered him his horse, which was refused. Lieut Jenkins took Sergt.-Farrier Hunt's stirrup, but after running a short distance he fell. By this time the enemy was quite close, but Private Herbert rode back to Lieut. Jenkins, who refused all assistance, and ordered Private Herbert to rejoin his squadron. As the enemy were now practically all round him, he would certainly have been taken prisoner if he had stayed any longer, so he galloped back to his troop, after having been under a heavy fire at close quarters for some minutes. For this act he was mentioned in despatches.

Lient. Jenkins, who, in falling, had hurt his hip, was taken prisoner. He was released on October 6th, and rejoined the Regiment on November 1st, at Heidelberg.

Major Smithson reported to the Officer Commanding as follows:—

> "Private Cooke, who was hit alongside of me, behaved very well, as also did the others.
>
> "Our casualties on this day were:
> One man killed.
> Major Smithson and one man wounded.
> Lieut. Jenkins missing.
> Four horses killed.
> Sixteen horses wounded.
>
> "Lieut. Church, who left with two troops of A to relieve Lieut. Wise and his two troops at Donga Spruit, was opposed by a considerable number of Boers, who galloped down to the line, and blew up a culvert near Wessel's Farm, doing but little damage. Lieut. Church undoubtedly prevented further damage being done. When the Boers attacking Mathew's Farm retreated, this force retired, and Lieut. Church proceeded to Donga Spruit."

This, by information gained later, and confirmed after peace, was to have been the main attack, and to have ended in the capture of Newcastle, in fact the Boers who numbered about 2,000 under Commandant Oppermann, were so sure of success that they wired that Newcastle had been captured. This wire appeared in some Dutch papers in Europe. The Boers subsequently accounted for this failure by the fact that one commando, under a distinguished commandant (Lucas Meyer), arrived too late, and the result was that they were beaten in detail.

The G.O.C. complimented Colonel Blagrove on the excellent work done by the Regiment during the day.

Major Smithson was invalided home in October, and rejoined the Regiment again in August, 1901.

On the 22nd, a 12-pounder gun was sent out to Sikafu, and was successfully got up the hill, and mounted during the night, and on the following day another 12-pounder was mounted on Windsor Castle.

On the 24th, about 8 a.m., the Boers again attacked the Royal's troop at Duck Pond Farm, and drove them in, at the same time showing a force with a pom-pom against our post at Donga Spruit. The 12-pounder that had been mounted on Sikafu on the 22nd, knocked out the pom-pom on Whitestone Ridge the first shot, and Donga Spruit was not bothered again while we held it.

The Boers advanced and occupied the heights to the north-west of Tendega, at the same time detaching a party, who took away with them 100lbs. of dynamite, a number of detonators, and a mule wagon, and span of mules from the collieries.

The Boers were forced to retire at 11.30 a.m., by their flank being turned on the south by the Royals, and on the north by a force under Colonel Blagrove, consisting of one squadron, 13th Hussars, two guns, R.F.A., and one company of the Middlesex Regiment.

On the 24th, the Officer Commanding Defences, Col. W. Hill, Middlesex Regiment, decided to relinquish Mathew's Farm as a night out-post, and the advanced half-squadron, which occupied that place, was ordered to retire every evening to the plate-layers' hut, near the Spur of Windsor Castle. Mathew's Farm was to be occupied at dawn daily, and held as before.

On the 25th, our patrol only saw six Boers, all told.

On the 26th, 2nd Lieut. Lambert went to hospital. He was subsequently invalided home, and rejoined the Regiment again in April, 1901.

August 27th, the Regiment turned out at 11.30 a m, under the following orders --

"The available cavalry will leave here (Newcastle), at 11.30 a.m. supported by two companies of infantry, and two guns, R.F.A., the latter to move at first to the ridge under Windsor Castle, and afterwards with your (O.C. Defences) direction to cover Wool's Drift. The Royals at Rooi Pynt have been ordered to support on the right by Dick's Drift, and to push patrols towards Utrecht."

In accordance with the above, the half-squadron at

Mathew's Farm was ordered to proceed to Wool's Drift, and sent a patrol on to Middlesex Hill. C Squadron and Head Quarters proceeded to Wool's Drift, and placed an observation post on Umbana.

The half-squadron under Lieut. Church, at Donga Spruit, sent a patrol to Doornkop, and a troop under Lieut. Bayley, temporarily lent by General Burn-Murdoch, to the sangar on the south-east end of Whitestone Ridge.

A patrol from C Squadron (Corporal Crook and six men) was sent to reconnoitre towards Welgevonden, proceeding between Doornkop and Umbana. After proceeding about two miles this patrol was driven in.

Another patrol (Corporal McElhannen and two men) was sent out in the same direction, but was also driven in. Lieut. Denny, who was ordered to stay out with an observation post, to see these patrols in, came under a somewhat heavy fire. The half-squadron from Donga Spruit reconnoitred all round Doornkop, seeing about 40 Boers, who were covering a larger force, but what it was could not be ascertained. Having collected all these parties, and having discovered the presence of the enemy on and near Bastion Hill, the Regiment retired about 5.30 p.m.

On the 28th and 29th no Boers were seen. About midnight, 28th—29th, a heavy train, while passing the platelayers' hut, fired the grass with sparks from the engine. About 20 horses and also 4 chargers stampeded. All these horses were recovered during the next day, but most of them were badly cut by barbed wire.

In a despatch dated November 9th, 1900, General Sir R. Buller, detailing the work of the force employed in safeguarding the lines of communications from Ladysmith to Heidelberg, from July to September, and in mentioning General Burn-Murdoch's name, says that his excellent arrangements and rapidity of movements secured the town and district of Newcastle from invasion, though it was, on many occasions, seriously attacked by superior forces, and notably on August 20th, 21st, 22nd, and 29th. The names of the following Officers, N.C.O.s, and men appeared in the despatch: —Bt.-Colonel H. J. Blagrove, Major Smithson, Lieut. L. Wise, Captains E. A. Wiggin, J. H. Tremayne (adjt.), A. H. Taylor, Lieut. E. W. Denny, S.S.M. Prentice, Privates Pritchard, Farrance, Herbert.

On September 3rd, Captain Ogilvy and Lieut. Spencer joined from England. Lieut. Spencer had been invalided home after going to hospital in January.

On September 5th, the troops at Newcastle acted in conjunction with Generals Hildyard and Talbot-Coke.

The information that we received was:—

"General Hildyard is to move from Volksrust on Wakerstroom early on the 15th instant, taking the road north of the hills which form the north boundary of Volksrust-Wakerstroom defile, so as to approach Wakerstroom from north-west direction.

"General Talbot-Coke's troops will, on the same day move from Ingogo in the direction north-

SOUTH AFRICAN WAR. 43

east side of Doornsfrand, to the west of Wool's Drift-Wakerstroom road.

"It is the intention of the G.O.C. (Burn-Murdoch), to demonstrate by Wool's Drift Bridge to Utrecht, in order to prevent the enemy's forces in that direction from reinforcing Wakerstroom."

Some slight confusion was caused at the commencement of these operations by the different forces working by different times. General Hildyard and General T. Coke were working by Cape time, while we were working by Natal time, a difference of over 30 minutes.

The force that left Newcastle consisted of one squadron 13th Hussars, three squadrons Royal Dragoons, under Colonel Blagrove; half-battalion Middlesex Regiment, four guns R.F.A., half-section field hospital, under Colonel Hill.

The two troops of A Squadron left the platelayers' hut, and were at the junction of the Ingagane and Nkandu Rivers by day-break, watching the right flank, and afterwards proceeding to Pamelo's Drift.

The two troops from A at Donga Spruit watched our left flank, taking up a position on Whitestone Ridge, and reconnoitring Doornkop.

C Squadron sent out one troop at 5 a.m. to Mathew's Farm, and patrolled towards Donga Spruit and Wool's Drift.

The remainder of Colonel Blagrove's force left camp at 6.30 a.m. Three troops of the Royals were on our right. At 8.40 a.m. we occupied Umbana and Middlesex Hill.

At 1.30 p.m., the Boers, in small parties, came on towards Umbana from the east, probably to try and find out if we had guns. There was brisk firing at long range for about ten minutes, when the Boers retired.

The Infantry and Artillery, who had been on Smithson's Ridge all day came on to Umbana in the evening, and bivouacked. C Squadron and the Royals bivouacked at Umbana. Major Williams' two troops near Pamelo's Drift, Lieut. Church's two troops under Whitestone Ridge.

On the 6th, information was received from General T. Coke, at Pimple Hill, about 8 a.m., that he wished our force to operate towards Welgevonden, along the south-east of Doornkop.

Bastion Hill was held by a few Boers, and the guns from Umbana fired a few shots at them, which drove them further back along the hill. About 4.45 p.m. a staff officer from General T. Coke rode over, and shortly after we retired to Umbana, and bivouacked.

On the 7th, we left Umbana at 8.30 a.m., and were ordered to search the country carefully as far as the foot of the berg, especially where the track leads up to the top of the berg, above Welgevonden Farm.

C. Squadron occupied Bastion Hill, and were later in the day relieved by the Infantry.

About 12 noon a squadron of the Royals galloped on, and fired on 80 to 100 Boers, but at a long range. Their movements were much hampered by a series of wire fences.

Welgevonden Farm, said to be a hospital, and flying red cross flags, on examination looked suspicious. The only patient was an idiot boy, the medical appliances were nil, and the paint of the red crosses on the wagons was still wet.

General T. Coke burnt Boreman's Farm.

On the 8th, sent patrols out in the morning, and about 11 a.m. the Douga Spruit and platelayers' hut half squadrons were ordered to retire to their respective posts, and C Squadron and Headquarters returned to Newcastle.

On the 9th, we were suddenly ordered out from Newcastle for Umbana. We left at 9 a.m., and found Umbana and Bastion Hill clear, but that there were a few snipers about was proved by Private Trustram being hit in the arm.

On the 10th, we were on and around Bastion Hill most of the day. The Royals advanced to the Berg, and within a mile of Utrecht, without seeing any of the enemy. We bivouacked as before.

The next day we advanced on Utrecht, and by 11.40 a.m. the scouts had been round and beyond the town and at 2 p.m. we got helio communication with Gen. Hildyard, who had met with but slight opposition.

We bivouacked about two miles west of Utrecht.

On the 12th, we left at 12.30 p.m., and returned to Umbana.

On the 13th a force consisting of three troops

(A Squadron) 13th Hussars, two companies Middlesex Regiment, under Major Close, remained at Umbana, The remainder of the Regiment returned to Newcastle, and Lieut. Church, with one troop returned to Donga Spruit. After this the Regiment was employed in seeing convoys through to Utrecht, via Umbana, and patrolling from Donga Spruit and from Newcastle to the berg on the west.

On the 14th, Lieut. Bayley returned to the staff.

On the 16th a patrol was fired on from Welgevonden Farm, which still had a red cross flag flying, and the next day it was blown up by General Hildyard's orders.

On the 22nd, an enormous swarm of locusts came over the camp. A very high wind was blowing, and the locusts were driven against the horses with considerable force. The men had to stand to the horses most of the afternoon.

October 1st, A Squadron reconnoitred Monkey Pass, and Donovan's Farm, in co-operation with the troops from Ingogo. No Boers were seen, and they returned to camp about 3.30 p.m.

Captain Battye arrived from B Squadron, on being transferred to A Squadron.

On October 3rd, 2nd Lieuts. Twist, Marchant, and Hodgkinson were promoted Lieutenants.

One troop was detached to occupy Fort Biddulph.

On the 8th, the District Commissioner of Utrecht having requested that the top of the Belalas Berg might be cleared, Colonel Blagrove was ordered to take a force which consisted of two squadrons 5th Dragoon Guards, two troops the Royals, six troops 13th Hussars to perform this duty. This force rendezvoused at Bezedenhout's Farm at 8.15 a.m., and spent the whole day in a very rough and precipitous country, collecting stock and clearing farms. A strong patrol of the 5th Dragoon Guards was fired on, and two men hit. The Boers cleared when they saw the squadron coming up.

Altogether 40 horses, 80 cattle, and 1,100 sheep were driven in, the troops returning to Umbana at 9 p.m.

On October 11th, Lieut. Marchant rejoined.

Between the 5th and the 15th, the weather was very bad, and the dust storms horrible.

On the 15th October, Sir Redvers Buller passed through Newcastle for Durban, on his way home.

On October 26th, it was reported that the Boers had burnt Waschbank station, and destroyed the line the previous night.

A Squadron, under Major Williams, left at noon for Dannhauser, arriving about 5 p.m., and there learned that the Boers were advancing north towards One Tree Hill, and would bivouac there. Major Williams wired to Newcastle, asking that the squadron of the Royals that was being sent by rail to Glencoe might co-operate with him at dawn the next morning at One Tree Hill, and received a reply that this should be done. At 3 a.m. the next morning A Squadron marched to One Tree Hill, arriving there at 5.30

a.m., but the Boers had gone three hours before over the berg.

There being no sign of the squadron of the Royals Major Williams waited till 8.30 a.m., and then started to return to Dannhauser. Just after starting he was called up. by the Royals' helio, from the place they should have been at 5 a.m., and informed that they were going after the Boers. Major Williams replied that they had left before his arrival, but received another message saying they would go on, and asking for his support. He followed the Royals for about eight miles, but nothing was seen of the Boers, Major Williams had received orders from General Hildyard this morning to hold the railway, and only send patrols out, but he took the squadron, thinking to make a capture, and that every man might be required.

On the 29th, A and C Squadrons concentrated at Newcastle, and on the 30th entrained for Greylingstad, Waterval, Vlakfontein for Eden Kop, and Heidelberg. On arrival the strength of the different detachments on November 1st were as under:—

Heidelberg:
  Colonel Blagrove, Commanding.
  Captain J. H. Tremayne, adjutant.
  Lieut. E. W. Denny, acting quarter master.
  Lieut. F W. Jarvis, Transport Officer.
  Captain McLaughlin, R.A.M.C.
  Lieut. Houston, A.V.D.
  3 troops of C Squadron, Capt. A. H. R. Ogilvy.
  Lieut. F. H. Wise.
  Lieut. G. H. Hodgkinson.

SOUTH AFRICAN WAR.

Lieut. C. E. Jenkins.
Lieut. F. W. U. Cosens.
Lieut. Clutterbuck (4th Hussars).
1 W.O., 161 N.C.O.'s and Men, 132 troop horses, 30 chargers.

Eden Kop:
1 Troop of C Squadron, Lieut. Lyons.
28 N.C.O.'s and Men, 26 horses, 3 chargers.

Greylingstad:
Major C. Williams.
Lieut. H. J. Stern.
Lieut. T. H. S. Marchant.
80 N.C.O.'s and Men, 72 horses, 8 chargers.

Waterval:
Major M. A. Close, 2nd in Command.
Captain L. R. S. Battye.
Lieut. J. F. Church.
Lieut. A. W. Spencer.
70 N.C.O.'s and Men, 63 horses, 11 chargers.

The strength of the B Squadron at Standerton was :—
Capt. E. A. Wiggin.
Lieut. A. Symons.
Lieut. W. Pepys.
Lieut. E. F. Twist.
2nd Lieut. L. B. B. Gubbins.
159 N.C.O.'s and Men, 152 horses.

The total strength of the Regiment at the front being :—
25 Officers, 1 Warrant Officer, 497 N.C.O.'s and Men, 445 horses.

The Boers at this time were very active in blowing up the line and holding up trains. The line was constantly patrolled by the Regiment, and also the irksome duties of escorting convoys, etc., and cattle guards fell to its lot.

The camp at Heidelberg was close to the station, where there was also an Army Service Corps depot, and consequently a considerable amount of stores. The defences round the station, considering the importance of the place, were decidedly weak. General Cooper, Commanding the Heidelberg Sub-District, authorised the employment of Kaffir labour, and, with their assistance, Captain Ogilvy's three troops in a short time made an attack by the Boers an event to be wished for.

Major Close, who took over command of Waterval had, besides the two troops of A Squadron, two companies Scottish Rifles, and two guns 64th Battery, R.F.A., under Lieut. Spiller. Here, also, it was found necessary to improve the defences, and this was proceeded with as rapidly as possible.

On November 4th, Lieut. Wise went down to Durban on his way home, on leave granted by Lord Roberts; and on May 4th, 1901, resigned his commission.

On November 8th, Captain Ogilvy took out 62 men from Heidelberg, leaving at 4 a.m., and proceeded to the Nigel mines, and from there reconnoitred towards Boschmanskop. He came in contact with the enemy in considerable numbers, and retired on the Nigel.

On the same day Lieut. Lyons was ordered to take his troops out from Eden Kop, to examine a kloof, where some cattle were supposed to be concealed. The country was very precipitous, and when the section that Lieut. Lyons had taken on retired, about half-a-dozen Boers crept up, and fired on them, hitting Lieut. Lyons in the leg with a ricochet shot.

The next day he was sent up to hospital in Pretoria, and was subsequently invalided home. He sailed for South Africa again on May 31st, 1902, rejoined the Regiment at Pretoria.

On the 9th, the Boers attacked the Nigel, but the company of infantry that was holding the place repulsed the attack, and C Squadron, who had turned out from Heidelberg, returned after proceeding a short distance.

Lieut. Spencer took over command of the troop at Eden Kop, and 2nd Lieut. Jenkins took his place at Waterval, on the 12th.

On the 12th, Colonel Blagrove was placed in command of all troops garrisoning Heidelberg town, and its immediate neighbourhood.

Lieut. Clutterbuck, 4th Hussars, left to rejoin his regiment in India.

On the 11th and 15th, the Boers attacked Vaal Station, about three miles from Waterval—on both occasions by night. These attacks were repulsed by the Scottish Rifles, under Capt. Barton, who only had two casualties.

All available troops from Greylingstad—A Squadron, 13th Hussars and Scottish Rifles—turned out to operate against Horne's Farm. A farm in the vicinity was blown up, but Horne's Farm itself was found to be strongly held in a very snug position. On retiring back to camp, the force was followed up, but suffered no casualties.

On the 18th, C Squadron were out most of the day watching the front, while the post at Houtpoort was being established. There were plenty of Boers about, but they went back to the hills, and though there was a certain amount of sniping throughout the day, there were no casualties.

On the 19th, one of the posts at Waterval was attacked by a party of about 16 Boers. No. 3400 Pte. Elsegood was wounded in the leg, and his horse shot. No. 4621 Pte. Elliott's horse was also killed, and he was injured by the horse rolling on him. These Boers were driven off by another post on the left.

Lieut. Stern, with his troop, went out reconnoitring from Greylingstad, and was attacked by about 70 Boers. He, however, extricated his troop with skill, and beyond having two horses hit, suffered no casualties. No. 3057 Corporal Jackson behaved with coolness and decision on this occasion, and his name was submitted to the Officer Commanding for early promotion. He was promoted sergeant on the 24th.

On the 20th, Major Williams took his squadron, and some of the Scottish Rifles to Daas Poort, and returned the same evening

On the 23rd, this force made a demonstration towards

SOUTH AFRICAN WAR.

the gold mine south east of Greylingstad, working in
conjunction with Colonel Bewicke-Copley's column

On the 24th, A Squadron, working with Colonel Bewicke-Copley's column, drove the Boers from Horne's Farm, and destroyed it.

Instead of there being 80 to 100 Boers at this farm, there were nearer 400.

During November, the Waterval detachment was busy clearing farms, and collecting provisions. This took some days, and there was always a certain amount of firing each day. Guide Waite, with his six native scouts, did good work during this time.

On the 26th, the 7th Dragoon Guards and 14th Hussars marched into Heidelberg, under Brigadier-General G. Hamilton.

Special precautions were taken by all the troops along the line to guard the railway until Lord Roberts had passed through on his way down country.

On the 29th, Lord Roberts published the following
  al Army Order:—

"Headquarters of the Army in South Africa.

"Johannesburg, 29th November, 1900."

"Being about to give up the command of the
 rmy in South Africa into the able hands of
 eneral Lord Kitchener of Khartoum, I feel
 cannot part with the comrades with whom
 have been associated for nearly a year
 -often under very trying circumstances—with-

out giving expression to my profound appreciation of the noble work they have performed for their Queen and country, and for me personally, and to my pride in the results they have achieved by their pluck and endurance, their discipline, and devotion to duty.

"I greatly regret that the ties which have bound us together are so soon to be severed, for I should like to remain with the Army until it is completely broken up, but I have come to the conclusion that as Lord Kitchener has consented to take over the command my presence is no longer required in South Africa, and that my duty calls me in another direction. But I shall never forget the officers and men of this force, be they Royal Navy, Colonials, Militia, Yeomanry, or Volunteers; their interests will always be very dear me, and I shall continue to work for the Army as long as I can work at all. The service which the South African force has performed is, I venture to think, unique in the annals of war, inasmuch as it has been absolutely almost incessant for a whole year, in some cases more than a year. There has been no rest days, no days off to recruit—no going into winter quarters, as in other campaigns which have extended over a long period. For months together, in fierce heat, in biting cold, and in pouring rain, you, my comrades, have marched and fought without a halt, and bivouacked without shelter from the elements, and you frequently have had to continue marching with your clothes in rags, and your boots without soles—time being of such great consequence that it was impossible for you to remain long enough in any one place to refit.

"When not engaged in actual battles you have been continually shot at from behind kopjes by an invisible enemy, to whom every inch of the ground was familiar, and who, from the peculiar nature of the country was able to inflict severe punishment while perfectly safe themselves.

"You have forced your way through dense jungles, and over precipitous mountains, through and over which, with infinite manual labour, you have had to drag and haul guns and ox wagons. You have covered with a most incredible speed, enormous distances, and that often on a very short supply of food, and you have endured the sufferings, inevitable in war, to sick and wounded men far from the base, without a murmur—even with cheerfulness. You have, in fact, acted up to the highest standard of patriotism, and by your conspicuous kindness, and humanity towards your enemies, and your forbearance and good behaviour in the towns we have occupied, you have caused the Army of Great Britain to be as highly respected, as it must henceforth be greatly feared, in South Africa.

"Is it any wonder that I am intensely proud of the Army I have commanded, or that I regard you—my gallant and devoted comrades—with affection as well as admiration, and that I feel deeply the parting from you? Many of you Colonials as well as Britishers—I hope to meet again; but those I may never see more will live in my memory, and be held in high regard to my life's end.

"I have learnt much during the war, and the experience I have gained will greatly help me in the work that lies before me, which is, I conceive, to make the Army of the United Kingdom as perfect as it is possible for any Army to be. This I shall strive to do with all my might. And now, farewell. May God bless every member of the South African Army, and that you may be all spared to return to your homes, and to find those dear to you well and happy, is the earnest hope of your commander,

"ROBERTS (Field-Marshal)."

The workers at Messrs. J. P. Coates' factory, Glasgow, sent the Regiment a large quantity of socks, tobacco, cocoa, etc. This generous and kindly gift which was very much appreciated, was received during the month.

Early in December the Boers were particularly active in destroying the line wherever they could.

On the 7th, 70 men from C Squadron marched out at 12.30 a.m., and joined a force under Lient.-Col. Bewicke-Copley, consisting of 250 King's Royal Rifles, and two guns, and marched to a ridge overlooking Deepkloof.

The forces under General G. Hamilton and Col. Colville, who had marched earlier in the night, were acting in co-operation, and it was hoped that the Boers in Kloof would be surrounded. However, the operations

SOUTH AFRICAN WAR.

were not successful. The next day was occupied in clearing farms, and several women and children were brought in, returning to Heidelberg in the evening.

This was always an unpleasant duty, but on this occasion the women were particularly annoying and troublesome. One of them who insisted on being brought in going to the length of giving birth to a child on a wagon during the journey.

On the 8th, the Boers destroyed the line near Vlaklaagte, and held up a train. Lieut. Church turned out with his troop from Waterval, but found the Boers had cleared. Shortly after, Capt. Wiggin and B Squadron arrived from Stauderton, but the Boers had a long start, and nothing could be done.

Sergt. Hetherington did very well on this morning. His duty was to patrol towards Vlaklaagte every morning, starting at 4.15. On this morning he heard firing beyond this point, and pushing on, opened fire on the Boers, causing them to retreat, and though he could not prevent them from driving off about 100 horses, he saved two truck loads of horses. The engine driver of this train was slightly wounded. The Boers tried to drive off some ponies from Waterval, but did not succeed, and lost a man wounded.

On the 13th, the Boers again derailed a train near Vlaklaagte, but were kept off by the escort of Kitchener's Fighting Scouts, who had two men injured when the train left the rails. No. 3583 Sergeant Hetherington's patrol again came up, and assisted in . . . , the Boers off. Lieut. Jenkins, with a troop from Waterval, and troops from Standerton, turned out but arrived too late.

General Wynne informed Major Williams that he was very pleased with Sergt. Hatherington's conduct on these occasions.

On the 15th, Lieut. A. Symons sailed for England to join the Staff College.

On the 18th, A Squadron received rifles in exchange for carbines, B Squadron got theirs on the 21st, and C Squadron got theirs on the 25th.

A party of one N.C.O. and six men were attached to the Infantry post at Frischgevaad—about seven miles out from Heidelberg.

On the 19th, No. 4984 Pte. Lee was wounded while patrolling from this post.

On the 24th, Lieut. Marchant, with a troop of A Squadron from Greylingstad, joined the mobile column under Colonel Colville, rejoining at Greyingstad early in January.

On the 24th, half the Eden Kop troop, under Lieut. Hodgkinson, went out with 150 men of the 2nd Devons and one pom-pom, for a foraging expedition, the whole under Captain Vigors, 2nd Devons, who reported as follows:—

hen seven miles out from Eden Kop, and whilst the wagons (eight) were loading, about 100 Boers attempted to surround my party.

"My left guard of 50 men, 2nd Devons, had got further than I intended, leaving a gap between the main body and them. That the Boers did not break through this gap was largely due, I consider, to the excellent work done by a party of the Cavalry.

"The party covering the wagons were attacked by about 40 Boers. They were warned by a scout, Pte. Blackley, 13th Hussars, that the enemy were advancing. He dismounted and assisted in the attempt to repel the Boers, and when matters got critical, mounted and brought away Corpl. Warmacott, 2nd Devons, clinging to his stirrup. Corpl. Warmacott informed me that had it not been for Pte. Blackley's assistance, he could not have got away. From the fact that the covering party had three killed, three wounded, and ten taken prisoners, I am of opinion that the conduct of this man deserves special mention.

No. 4145 Pte. Blackley was mentioned in dispatches.

On December 29th, the line was torn up near Vaal, and a supply train, with a quantity of canteen stores, was derailed. The Boers, who had probably between 200 and 300 strong, looted the train, and then set fire to it. Lieut. Church, with his troop, turned out from Waterval, and half company of Scottish Rifles came out from Vaal. Lieuts. Stern and Marchant with their troops, and a company of Mounted Infantry from Colonel Colville's Column at Greylingstad, also turned out, but the Boers retired, and nothing more than long range firing took place.

On December 16th, Lieut. Jarvis and 30 men of C Squadron left Heidelberg, to join Colonel Colville's Column at Modderfontein (326) on the Zuicherbosch

River. The column, which was about 600 strong, consisted of :—

  1st Batt. Rifle Brigade.
  63rd Battery, R.F.A. (Major C. H. de Rougemont).
  1 pom-pom (Captain Patch).

The next morning the column advanced in the direction of Malan's Kraal (73), and, in consequence of there being no other mounted troops the work this troop had to perform was very difficult, the 30 men having to furnish advance, rear, and flank guards. Col. Colville's orders were to clear the country between the line and the Vaal, and to work down to Standerton.

There were several small parties of Boers, and the troop was daily engaged.

On the 17th, the advance guard was temporarily checked by a superior force, and No. 4063 Lce.-Corpl. Bradley was wounded, and fell from his horse. No. 3352 Pte. Dempster galloped up to his assistance under a heavy fire, and took him up on his own horse, and afterwards sent him in to the ambulance, while he himself walked into the advanced company of the column. For this gallant action Pte. Dempster was mentioned in despatches.

On the 18th the Column marched to Grootvlei (76), and halted there the next day. Lieut. Jarvis was sent with a patrol of about 12 men, and found a strong party of Boers holding a ridge close to camp. Two companies of infantry were sent out, and the Boers were driven from the ridge, but they were very soon strongly reinforced, and a sharp skirmish ensued before they were driven off. No. 3181 Pte. McMasters was wounded, and two horses were hit.

On the 20th, the column marched to Leeuwspruit (138) camping above Kalk Spruit. By this time the supplies for the column were running short, as the convoy which it had been arranged should have been sent out to Modderfontein (326), had not arrived, so Lieut. Jarvis was sent into Vlakfontein to get information concerning it. On arriving there he was informed that orders had been received that the convoy was not to proceed without an escort of at least three companies of Infantry, and as this force was not available it had not been possible to send the convoy to the column. Lieut. Jarvis returned to Vlakfontein, and reported to Col. Colville, who decided to take his column into Vlakfontein.

On the 21st, the column marched at 5.30 a.m., in a thick fog, which cleared off when it had marched about half way. A force of about 400 Boers was almost immediately discovered by our advanced scouts, concealed behind a small kopje. A sharp fight took place, lasting till about 12.30 p.m. The column reached Vlakfontein about 2 p.m.

On the 23rd, the column marched out to the South Rand mine, and the following day a start was made to attack the north-west corner of the Rooi Kopjes. The Boers had a fine natural position, and very little way could be made against them. The two farms at the foot of the hills were burnt, however.

During the day Lieut. Marchant and a troop of A Squadron joined the column from Greylingstad.

The next day being Christmas Day, the column rested, and prepared for the fun on Boxing Day.

On December 26th, another attempt was made to drive the Boers from the Rooi Kopjes—this time rather more to the west. One company of the Rifle Brigade, under Captain Radclyffe, with one pom-pom (Major Harvest), which had joined at Vlakfontein was left to guard the camp. Lieut. Marchant's troop found the advance and right flank guard and Lieutenant Jarvis' troop found the rear and left flank guard. The right flank guard soon came under a heavy fire from some Boers concealed in a donga, who bolted on the guns coming into action. An advance was then made and a farm was destroyed about a mile from the kopjes, the Boers mking a strong resistance, and several casnalties occurred among the Rifle Brigade. At the same time several parties of Boers were seen galloping away, and disappearing over the ridge behind Commandant Buys' house, and suspicion was aroused that they intended getting round our flanks, and attacking the camp, which was about five miles distant. This was reported to Colonel Colville twice before 10 a.m., and a message was sent into the camp.

About 1 p.m. it was discovered that these suspicions were correct, and that the Boers were attacking the camp. The column retired, being followed up from the hills, and were in time to drive the Boers off.

The pom-pom, which had remained in camp, had all its horses shot, and had to be run in by hand to prevent its being taken. Major Harvest was wounded, Captain Radclyffe was also wounded, and the total casualties during the day was close on 70 men killed and wounded, about two-thirds of this number being those who remained in camp.

About 8.30 p.m., an attack was made on the camp, but the outposts were sufficient to keep the enemy off.

Th column marched about 8.30 a.m., the following morning to Greylingstad, and on the 30th Liqut. Jarvis' troop returned to Heidelberg by rail.

With reference to the fight on the 21st, the summary of news contained the following:—

"Col. Colville, with moveable column, engaged two separate commandoes on the 21st near Vlakfontein. Enemy retired before our attack when Infantry was within 600 yards of their position, and lost several men. Our casualties, three wounded. Colonel Colville attributes small loss to excellent shooting of 63rd Battery, and skilful leading of Lieut. Jarvis, 13th Hussars, Captain Talbot, and 2nd Lieutenant White, Rifle Brigade.

"Col. Colville was attacked by the enemy on the same day at Modderfontein. The engagment lasted from 9 a.m. to 12.30 p.m., when the enemy retired."

Lady Russell had again shown her kindly interest in the Regiment by collecting comforts, etc., for the men, and Colonel and Mrs. Spilling very kindly sent a handsome present of pipes and tobacco.

Nor did our comrades in the Reserve Squadron forget us. They sent out a generous supply of puddings, which we ought to have got by Christmas, but did not get till January. The kindness of those at home was much appreciated.

The strength of the Regiment at the front on December 31st, 1900, was:—

21 Officers, 1 W.O., 452 N.C.O.'s and Men, 407 horses.

Wanting to complete:—

5 Officers, 54 N.C.O.'s and Men, 46 horses.

Army Orders received on December 31st contained the following message from Her Most Gracious Majesty:—

"From V.R.I. to Lord Kitchener.

"My heart-felt good wishes to you and all ranks under your command for Christmas and the New Year."

During the year 1900 the deaths in the Regiment were as follows:—

Killed in action	2
Died of wounds	1
Enteric	27
Dysentry	6
Drowned	1
Other causes	3
	40

And 201 men have been invalided home. The drafts from England amounted to 221 N.C.O.'s and men.

The Boers were round Heidelberg in no great numbers, and were not very active. However, they were continually worrying the cattle guards, and sniping patrols when they could do so with safety.

On the 5th, Boers were reported in and about Glads Farm, about two miles to the west of the town. Captain Ogilvy took out 40 men, and a gun, and a few Mounted Infantry supported him. When he got to the ridge beyond the farm he came under fire, and lost a horse. The Boers retired to the hills, where they were quite safe.

On the 5th January, Lieut. C. O. Dangar, from the 3rd Battalion West Riding Regiment, was gazetted to the Regiment, but was retained for duty with the Army Service Corps.

On the 16th, a party of Boers came down to Klippoortjie, about 2 a.m., and drove off a few cattle belonging to the Kaffirs. The Kaffirs said there were about 200 of the enemy. This place was about a mile-and-a-half outside the town.

On the 17th, the S.A.C. began forming a Depot at Heidelberg. Their camp was on our left.

The Greylingstad and Waterval detachments were similarly employed during the month.

On the 6th Captain McLoughlan, R.A.M.C., left us.

Sub-District Orders, 23/1/01.

"The General Officer Commanding very much regrets to notify to all ranks in this sub-district the following telegram, and he feels sure all will join him in sincere sympathy with the Royal Family in their great sorrow.

"From Chief, Pretoria.

"An official announcement of the death of her Majesty the Queen at 6.30 yesterday has been received.

On the 26th, the following special order was received:—

"The following telegram has been received from Edward R. by Lord Kitchener."

"Am much touched by your kind telegram of sympathy, and beg you to convey my warmest thanks to my gallant Army in South Africa."

The following reply has been sent by Lord Kitchener to His Majesty the King.

"Your Majesty's gracious telegram has been communicated to the troops. On behalf of the Army in South Africa I humbly beg to express our feelings of the utmost loyalty and devotion to your Majesty."

The accession of His Majesty King Edward VII. was proclaimed in London on the 24th inst.

During the last days of January and during February, the Boers came down in small parties to try and get cattle, almost daily from Heidelberg. However, they did not succeed, nor did they do any damage, beyond wounding a horse or two.

The amount of cattle, sheep, and goats, at Heidelberg at this time was enormous, and they died in hundreds, especially during the end of February and beginning of March, when the weather was very bad. Consequently, it was very difficult to keep the place

SOUTH AFRICAN WAR. 67

sanitary. The neighbouring Kaffirs had all been collected in a location just outside the town on the Nigel Road, and their presence hardly added to the sanitary state of the place. There was also a small community of surrendered burghers in "Hands up Dorp," a short distance beyond the Kaffirs. One of these burghers was detected (February 17th) in taking a Mauser and a quantity of ammunition out of the Blesbok Spruit.

On February 2nd, 60 men of A Squadron, from Greylingstad, under Major Williams, escorted a convoy to Waterval, and were lucky in not coming in conflict with the Boers in superior numbers, as 300 crossed the line near Groot Pan about an hour before the convoy got there.

On the 4th, Lieut Jenkins went to hospital in Pretoria with enteric. He rejoined the Regiment on May 11th

On the 6th the up mail was held up at Vlakfontein. The Greylingstad detachment turned out, and got to the train, a distance of 10 miles, within an hour of the information being received, but the Boers had cleared off.

The next day the line was destroyed near Vlaklaagte, and the down mail held up. The Waterval detachment turned out, and watched the derailed train during the day. About 80 Boers were seen, but though there was a little firing they did not come on. The line was considerably damaged, and when the construction train came up, it exploded a dynamite cartridge which the mail had passed over without exploding. A deviation had to be made, and traffic was stopped till about 2 p.m. the following day. The next train that came up, about 2 p.m., was derailed about two-and-a-half miles from Waterval by dynamite. The line was not cleared till about 4 p.m. the following day. The Waterval detachment was out all day, guarding the train, which was a supply train.

On the 6th, B Squadron marched to Waterval, en route to Greylingstad, where they arrived the next day, but on the 10th they were sent back to Standerton.

On the 13th the Boers blew up a culvert, just west of Groot Spruit. A Squadron turned out from Greylingstad, and drove the Boers off the wrecked train, only giving them time to take a few sacks of sugar. This squadron picked up two rifles, and three bandoliers, and found two Boer ponies dead, so it is presumed that the Boers had some casualties. The Scottish Rifles came out on wagons, and relieved the Greylingstad detachment.

On the 15th, the Greylingstad detachment was called out to Vlakfontein, where a large force of Boers had crossed during the night. They returned to Greylingstad in the evening.

On the 20th, about 12.30 p.m., the up mail train near Botha's Krall, while going slowly up an incline, exploded a mine under the centre of the train, derailing two coaches, and bringing the train to a standstill. Captain Wiggin, who was coming up to Heidelberg, was the senior officer on the train, and had with him about 15 men of the Devons as train escort, and 15 Grenadier Guards, who were going up to join

SOUTH AFRICAN WAR.

the Johannesburg Police. As soon as the train was
brought to a standstill, the Boers opened fire from a
kopje about 400 yards to the left of the train. The
men immediately got off the train, and lined the side
of the railway, but in doing so the Devons had four
men hit, and the Guards had one man hit, and two
Kaffirs were also hit, while one of the Devons broke
his leg in jumping off the truck. The gun from Botha's
Krall opened fire at a range of about 3,000 yards,
and shortly afterwards the 5in. gun from Eden Kop
commenced to shell the Boers, at a range of about
five and a half miles. The first two shells dropped
midway between the train and the Boers, and the
third shell fell right on the kopje on which the Boers
were. This caused the Boers to retire to another
kopje about 900 yards from the train, which was a
great relief, as up to now their fire had been unpleasantly accurate. About 1.30 p.m. the armoured train
arrived from Vlakfontein, and opened fire with a
pom-pom.

As soon as the news was received at Heidelberg
that the train was held up, as many of our men as
possible were turned out, this amounted to about 20,
as all the others were on duty. 40 K.R.R.'s on wagons were also sent out, and about 25 S.A.C. About
5.30 p.m. Capt. Wiggin got the armoured train up,
and pulled away the coaches in rear of the break in
the line, and connected the telephone to the wires,
and explained the situation to Heidelberg. The Heidelberg troops now began to get round the Boers, and
it became evident to them that their chance of getting that train had gone, so they galloped off. The
wounded men and women were taken back to Vlakfon-

tein in the coaches drawn out by the armoured train, and the construction train repaired the line in about one-and-a-half hours, and the train was got on to Heidelberg.

On February 23rd, the line was broken near Zuicherbosch, and on the 26th it was broken near Rietvlei. On neither occasion was much damage done.

On the 26th, one troop and 25 S.A.C. reconnoitred to Rietvlei, and from there went round by Marais Farm, but saw no sign of the enemy.

The strength of the Regiment at the front was:— 19 Officers, 1 Warrant Officer, 404 N.C.O.s and Men, 391 horses. Wanting to complete:—6 Officers, 102 N.C.O.s and Men, 62 horses.

The total number of N.C.O.'s and Men in the country was 529, 78 of whom were in various hospitals.

The weather during March was very bad. About the middle of the month it rained nearly continuously for a week.

On 6th March, about 11 p.m., the S.A.C. post on the first culvert up the line began firing heavily, and reported that some mounted Boers had come down towards the line, but had retired when fired on. There had been a good many false alarms about this time, indeed, later on during the night there was another.

The A.S.C. post on our right fired on the night soil cart. They did no damage, but it was hard lines on the old man, whose employment was not the most pleasant under the most favourable circumstances.

The next morning it turned out that the S.A.C. had

very likely seen Boers, as a fairly large party had come down to some huts occupied by Coolies and Kaffirs, near Klippoortjie, during the night. They robbed the Coolies of all their money, and called a Kaffir outside his hut, and then shot him through the face, blowing off one side of it.

The ganger and native workmen who left Rietvlei station at daybreak (on the 7th) on a trolley to patrol the line were blown up by a dynamite cartridge, about four or five miles from Heidelberg. The ganger himself, who was sitting in the front part of the trolley, was blown into the air, but was not much hurt. Three of the native workmen were killed, and the others shockingly injured. The construction train left Heidelberg about 9.30 a.m. to repair this damage, but after proceeding a very short distance it exploded another mine placed under a sleeper. Fortunately, very little damage was done.

On the 15th and 23rd, the Boers blew up a supply train near Vlaklaagte. On the 15th, they did not get anything, but on the 28th, they got a good haul of supplies, and took the escort, numbering 16 men, prisoners. The strength of the Boers was estimated at about 400, and on both occasions they had wagons with them to carry off the supplies.

On March 25th, Lieut. F. Jarvis, Loyal Suffolk Hussars, went to hospital at Elandsfontein with enteric, and to the regret of all, he did not come back to the Regiment. He was subsequently invalided home, and afterwards was given a commission in the S.A.C., and was promoted to be captain shortly after joining that corps

On the 28th, S.S.M. Holden, after having served in the Regiment for 21 years and 10 months, left Standerton for England for discharge on the expiration of his term of service.

On the 28th, Lieut Church's troop from Waterval joined Colville's Column, and during the evening took up a position just north of Vogelstruisfontein, with the object of preventing De Wet from crossing the line. The same positions were held the next day and night. About 10.30 p.m.. No. 3548, Corpl. Gavin, who was sent out with one man with a message to Colonel Colville was fired on by the Scottish Rifles, and wounded in the arm.

Lieut. Church's troop returned to Greylingstad on the 31st (vide B Squadron, page 91).

The strength of the Regiment at the end of March, 1901, was:—

At the front:—
18 Officers, 1 W.O., 392 N.C.O.'s and Men, 378 horses.

Wanting to complete:—
7 Officers, 114 N.C.O.'s and Men, 75 horses.

Total number of Men in South Africa, 508.

Total number of men in hospital, 72.

SOUTH AFRICAN WAR.

B SQUADRON.

May 7th, during the morning three troops of B Squadron marched from the regimental camp, Ladysmith, to Modderspruit, where they were joined by the fourth troop, which had been at Surprise Hill, with Clery's Division for the last month.

Captain Wiggin was in command of this squadron, and had with him Captain Battye, Lieutenants Symons, Pepys, and Twist. The strength of the squadron was 106 men and 113 horses.

The squadron was attached to Clery's Division as Divisional Cavalry.

May 8th, all tents and heavy baggage were sent back to Ladysmith.

May 9th, the force advanced with Sir R. Buller to attempt the turning of the Biggarsberg. For four days they marched through a rough bushy country, with no incident beyond the interchange of a few shots between the Boers' scouts and our advance guards.

May 13th, at Vermaak's Kraal, on the morning of the 13th, they were just breaking camp when the Boer gun on Helpmaakar Heights began to drop shells into our baggage. Our two 4.7's immediately replied, and with the third shot effectually silenced the Long Tom. During the day Dundonald's Brigade and the 2nd Infantry Brigade (Hamilton's) captured the Helpmaakar Ridges with trifling loss, the feeble attempt to stand made by the Boers being checkmated by the appearance of Bethune's Column from the east, he having worked round through Greytown, and the Umvoti country. The squadron was unfortunately detailed as escort to the supply column, so were unable to assist the Colonials in their pursuit along the Dundee Road.

May 14th, the following day they moved to Beith, where they awaited the arrival of the supply park from Waschbank.

May 15th, at 8 p.m., they marched for Dundee arriving at 2 a.m.

May 16th, the Boers had evacuated the town, and our Army was bivouacking about one mile on the northern side.

May 17th, after a day's rest, the force advanced and covered the 38 miles to Newcastle in two days. No opposition was met with en route.

May 19th, the Fourth Brigade (Cooper's) and Dundonald's Brigade pushed on to Mount Prospect and Ingogo, finding the Boers in position on Laing's Nek. The squadron halted at Newcastle, with the 2nd Brigade, till the 29th, then moved on to Ingogo Hill. During the ten days' halt the squadron made several reconnaissances towards the Buffalo, and on one occasion Lieut. Symons and a small patrol crossed the river at Wool's, the first of the 13th Hussars to enter the Transvaal.

Lieut. Pepys was sent to Dundee in charge of Boer prisoners, rejoining before the squadron left Newcastle.

SOUTH AFRICAN WAR. 75

May 29th, from the 29th May to June 16th, the squadron was employed on outpost duty at Ingogo. The Boers had a Long Tom on Pongwana, with which they annoyed the 4th Brigade at Mount Prospect, bursting shrapnel at 11,000 yards, but they could no reach our camp.

During Buller's flank march through Botha's Pass and Alleman's Nek, the squadron was escort to the heavy guns, and on June 16th marched with them to Laing's Nek, which position the Boers had left two days earlier.

June 19th, Buller moved on with his whole force, and Standerton was reached on the 24th. The only enemy encountered during the week being "winter and rough weather." Lieut. Pepys went sick with jaundice on the 20th, and was sent down to Durban.

After a week's rest at Standerton, the force again pushed on. Near Vaal the Boers ambushed a party of Strathcona's Horse, capturing about 10. Our rear guard had a slight brush on the 3rd near Groot Spruit, and had one horse killed.

July 5th, at Vlakfontein Buller's and Roberts' Army joined hands for the first time. General Hart, who had gone round the other side after the relief of Ladysmith, riding over from Zuicherbosch to meet Buller.

For the next three weeks the squadron trekked with Clery's Column, between Bethel and Greylingstad. A considerable number of Boers, under Pretorious and Buys hung on our flanks and rear every day. The squadron was permanent rearguard, and came in for a good deal of sniping, but suffered no loss beyond a few horses.

Lieut. Pepys rejoined the squadron on July 16th.

On July 19th, near Leeuw (Standerton), the Boers charged the squadron under cover of a grass fire. Two companies of the 60th came to its assistance, and the attack was soon beaten off. The 60th had one man killed.

On August 14th, Lieut. Gubbins and some men and horses arrived from the Regiment at Newcastle, bringing the strength of the squadron up to 6 officers, 142 N.C.O.'s and Men, and 140 horses. The month of August was spent at Greylingstad and Vlakfontein, and was altogether without incident.

At the end of the month the column returned to Standerton. The squadron then left the column, and formed part of the garrison. Their chief duties consisted of outposts, cattle guards, and clearing farms.

On September 20th, the Boers sniped out outpost at Rademeyer's Farm, and No. 3676 Pte. Brodrick was badly wounded in the leg.

Lieut. Twist's troop, which had been patrolling to Leeuw Spruit, was somewhat severely pressed by the enemy on their way home, having two horses killed. No. 3408 Pte. Pritchard distinguished himself by riding back under a heavy fire, and catching a horse which had broken loose, and brought it back to the troop. For this action he was mentioned in despatches.

November 28th, Lieut. Symons and half of the squadron was sent to Platrand to assist the Garrison there in reconnaisance.

SOUTH AFRICAN WAR.

The following day they came in contact with Britz Commando, and No. 4083 Pte. Lewis was wounded, and three horses hit.

The half squadron rejoined on the evening of November 2nd.

At 4 a.m., on December 2nd, Capt. Wiggin, who had with him the half-squadron at Standerton, and 150 M.I., 150 Infantry, and two guns moved out to clear a farm some ten miles to the east.

A strong force of Boers attempted to prevent them carrying off the meallies, and almost succeeded in cutting off a party of the T.M.I. Under cover, however, of the guns, Capt. Wiggin with some M.I., advanced on foot, and turned the enemy out of a krall, from which the enemy had been firing heavily. The enemy were ultimately driven off, and the force returned to Standerton with four wagon loads of mealies, etc.

No. 4107 Pte. Ware was slightly wounded in the face and No. 3776, Sergt. Mahon, who had taken on to his horse an officer of the T.M.I. who had been dismounted, had a heavy fall over wire, which incapacitated him for three months.

December 4th, the squadron with 70 M.I. and 200 Infantry, and two guns under Major Coghill, R.A., again had a sharp brush with the enemy whilst clearing a farm in the same vicinity. Two gunners were wounded but the squadron had no casualties.

December 13th, about 7.30 a.m., it was reported that the Boers had held up a train near Vlakfontein. The squadron made a very quick turn out, and arrived at the train, a distance of 11 miles, within an hour, but found the Boers had gone; and waited till the overturned trucks were got on the line, and then returned to Standerton.

On December 14th, Lieut. A. Symons left for Durban, en route for England, he having been granted a nomination at the Staff College.

December 21st, about 6 a.m., Pte. Pearson came galloping in, and reported that Rademeyer's picquet had been heavily attacked. It was very foggy, and the Boers had crept up under cover of the mist. The squadron saddled up, and on arriving at Rademeyer's Farm, the Boers were seen trekking away in the distance. The 4.7 gun on the kop sent a shell after them, but did not quite reach them. It appears that the Boers came suddenly out of the fog, and took Corpl. Willman and two men prisoners as they were patrolling in front of the post. After taking their arms and horses they let them go. They then attacked the post, but Ptes. Pike and Laggett held on, and hit two Boers. Pte. Pearson, who was alone in the right sangar, emptied his magazine before retiring, and a dead horse was found 30 yards in front of his post.

B Squadron received rifles in the place of carbines the same evening.

January 2nd, the sqaudron, with two companies infantry and two guns, under Captain Wiggin, made a reconnaisance towards De Lange's Drift. The rain and mist came on so thick that this force was obliged to turn back, after covering about 10 miles.

January 7th, about 2 p.m., received information

that the Boers had driven off some cattle which were grazing south of Standerton Kop. Half the squadron galloped out in pursuit, and exchanged shots with the Boer's rear-guard across the Vaal river, near Eloff's Farm (10 miles). As the Boers were in some force, and the half-squadron only consisted of forty men, it was impossible to force a crossing.

January 13th, the squadron marched at 1 a.m., with the second Divisional M.I., hoping to find Boers at Boschof's Farm, but drew blank, were again defeated by the heavy fog, so returned to camp.

January 14th, the squadron marched at 2 p.m., and joined Colville's column at Rietvlei, 15 miles north east of Standerton.

The column consisted of:—

    1 Squadron 13th Hussars.
    1 Squadron Mounted Infantry.
    50 Standerton Police.
    1st Battalion Rifle Brigade.
    Four guns 64th Battery R.F.A.
    1 pom-pom.

Strength about 1,200.

January 15th, on the following day the column moved towards Bethel, and found a large number of Boers on our front. The mounted troops consisting of the squadron, 1 Company M.I., and 50 Standerton Police, were engaged from 9 a.m. to 5 p.m. During the afternoon it was found necessary to charge a ridge. They were received with a hot fire, but the men behaved very steadily, and dismounting, rapidly drove the Boers back to Boschmanskop.

No. 4142 Pte. Brewer and No. 4887 Pte. Mitchell were wounded, and seven horses were hit.

During the course of the day No. 3550 Pte. Cleaver behaved with commendable coolness in catching Pte. Jennings' horse, and Pte. Snelling took Pte. Jennings on his horse and carried him back to the squadron.

The column camped that night at Van Staden's Dam.

A lamp message was received ordering Colonel Colville to march back to the line at once, and to entrain half the battalion Rifle Brigade at Vlaklaagte for Heidelberg.

January 16th, the column marched at 7 a.m. in the following formation:

    Advance Guard, Standerton Police.
    Main Body.
    Baggage with half-battalion R.B.
    Rear Guard.
    Artillery, half-battalion R.B.B., Squadron 13th Hussars, and M.I. half-squadron, under Lieut. Pepys, right rear, and half-squadron, under Lieut. Twist, left rear, and the M.I. and pom-pom in rear of the centre.

Shortly after leaving camp, the enemy began to press on our left-rear, and the M.I. and pom-pom went to support Lieut. Twist. Under cover of these demonstrations the Boers began to move round our right, and large masses appeared on the ridges to that hand. As the rear half-battalion and guns were crossing a vlei near Bosmanskranz the Boers suddenly jumped down on our right, our rear, and left rear,

Lieut. Pepy's half-squadron on the right held on in a pan for some little time, but were so hard pressed that they had to fall back, and took up a position on a small knoll between the infantry of the baggage guard, and that of the rear guard.

Lance-Corpl. Harding, who was out with a patrol on the extreme right, behaved with great gallantry, holding on to a ridge with two men, until the leading Boers were 200 yards from him, then mounting and galloping back to join Lieut. Pepys. His action caused some of the Boers to dismount and open fire, and so gained time for the rear-guard infantry, who formed to their right at the double, and just succeeded in reaching the top of the ridge as the Boers were riding up the other side. The enemy made a gallant attempt to get to close quarters, standing up in the open, and replying to the heavy fire of the R.B.s. However, when the latter fixed bayonets, and began to advance, they cried enough, and fled precipitately.

In the meantime the baggage guard and Pepys' on the little knoll, which practically connected the two half-battalions R.B., had come in for a warm time, but ultimately the steady fire of our men prevailed, and the Boers remounted and galloped off.

On the left-rear, Captain Wiggin, with Lieut. Twist's half-squadron, and the M.I. Company, had taken up a position on a round hill, protecting the left of the baggage, and the rear of the infantry, who had formed to the right.

The firing was heavy, but the grass was so long that very little damage was done on either side, and the

Boers, after trying for about half-an-hour to take the hill, drew off. Colonel Colville, being anxious about his baggage, and expecting another attack on our original front, which, but for a few police, was unprotected, then gave the order to draw in on the guns. The Boers, however, had had quite enough for one day, and beyond a little sniping attempted nothing further.

Our casualties were, Guide Allison (1 G.) killed, 12 R.B., 2 13th Hussars wounded, viz:—No. 3318 Pte. Sutton, and No. 3051 Pte. Pollock, and 1 M.I. wounded. Besides the two men above mentioned, Pte. Ware was very slightly wounded in the hand. Lieut. Pepys had a bullet through his helmet, and 7 horses were hit, including Captain Wiggin's horse. It was learnt afterwards from Boers who fought on that day that their casualties were about 50 killed and wounded, and that their force, numbering about 1,500, was composed of men from the Heidelberg, Bethel, Standerton, Ermelo, and Wakkerstroom Commandoes, under Chris. Botha, and Vecht General Spruyt.

Colonel Colville, in his report, said:—

> "I ascribe my success to the good handling of the baggage guard by Captain Talbot, R.B., of the mounted troops by Captain Wiggin, of the guns by Major Coghill."

He also, in a later despatch, especially mentioned Lieut. Pepys and Lance-Corpl. Harding.

In the afternoon the column moved on towards the line, and camped about four miles from Vlaklaagte, which station they reached at 8 a.m. the following morning (January 17th).

SOUTH AFRICAN WAR.

After a few hours' halt, the squadron, with the Standerton Police, left the column, and marched to Standerton.

January 28th, about 70 men of B Squadron and 40 Standerton Police, under Captain Wiggin, paraded at 9 p.m., and guided by Mr. Allison, resident magistrate, made a night march to a farm near Roberts' Drift, on the Vaal, about 18 miles distant. The night was very dark and wet, but by jogging along, the river was reached about 1 a.m. The banks were very steep and slippery, so crossing was not an easy matter. One man and horse rolled down about 30 feet into the water, though neither were hurt. However, after some delay, all got over except one troop, Lieut. Gubbins', which was left to hold the drift, and cover the retirement. After riding on about a mile, the natives told us that the farm was near at hand, so dismounting, we crept through a big mealie patch, and surrounded the house. Dashing open the door, we rushed in, and found seven Boers in bed. They made no resistance, and surrendered at once. Two natives who tried to escape were slightly wounded. In a krall close by, we found about a dozen ponies, and 50 cattle. We had some little trouble in finding our horses again, and, as it was still very dark when we reached the river, Captain Wiggin thought it advisable to wait for the first streak of dawn. We crossed at 3.30 a.m., and reached Standerton with the prisoners and loot at 7 a.m., having covered 35 miles in the 10 hours.

February 4th, the squadron paraded at 4.30 a.m., and marched out some 10 miles to the east, to bring in a convoy from Dartnell's Column. Mistaking us for Boers they turned a pom-pom on us, fortunately without doing any damage. Reached camp at noon.

February 5th, the squadron escorted the wagons back to Dartnell's Column.

February 6th, the squadron marched at 6.30 a.m. to Waterval.

February 7th, the squadron marched at 6.30 a.m. to Greylingstad, where the squadron was required to assist the A Squadron in patrolling, as the Boers had been very active in blowing up the line, and had held up several trains in that vicinity.

February 10th, the squadron marched at 9.30 a.m., back to Waterval. Captain Wiggin, having had a bad fall, returned to Standerton by train.

February 11th, marched at 3.45 a.m., and met a party of M.I., and two guns from Standerton, under Major Kayes, 60th Rifles. Reconnoitred to Joubert's Kop. On the way back to Standerton, the rear guard was attacked by 200 Boers, but, chiefly owing to the excellent shooting of the R.A., they were driven off, the only casualty being one M.I. wounded, and one horse hit.

February 13th, half the squadron, under Lieut. Pepys, went out to Welgedacht, and took over a convoy of Boer families from Colville, and escorted them back to Standerton. There was a little sniping on the left flank.

February 21st, a few Boers sniped the picquet at Grobelaar's Farm. The picquet replied, wounding one

Boer, whom his comrades carried off. They then retired.

February 23rd, an order was received to send a patrol of one N.C.O. and six men, to Boschman's kop, about six miles distant. As they were nearing the top of the hill they were fired on, and No. 3267 Pte. Heaps, the advanced scout, was hit, and knocked off his horse. The picquet at Rademeyer's Farm, hearing the firing, galloped out in support, and occupied the kop. As soon as the Boers saw this picquet coming they cleared off. An ambulance was sent out from Standerton to bring in Pte. Heaps, but he succumbed to his wound the same evening.

March 3rd, orders were received from the squadron to start for Vrede on the following day, with General Barr Campbell's Column. This column consisted of:—

    3rd Grenadier Guards.
    4th I.Y.
    4 Guns.
    1 pom-pom.

March 4th, marched at 5.30 a.m. to De Lange's Drift, seeing no Boers.

March 5th, marched at 5.30 a.m., with the squadron as rearguard, and reached Vrede about 5 p.m. For the last eight miles, the road ran through rough, hilly country, and some 200 Boers worried the flanks and rear guard all the way. The half squadron, under Lieut. Pepys, fired, on an average, 150 rounds per man. Several Boers were accounted for, and our only casualty was one I.Y. wounded.

From March 6th to 9th, it rained almost incessantly,

and the Column waited at Vrede for the weather to clear.

March 10th, the column marched at 6 a.m., and were accompanied by the 2nd Leinsters and two more guns. The squadron was not engaged, but the rear guard had a little skirmish, and two men of the Leinsters were wounded.

Camped at Mooi Bank.

March 11th, as the rain had come on with redoubled vigour, the drift over the spruit (Zonderdrift) was impassable. All that day the R.E. and Infantry were working hard to repair it.

March 12th, the squadron, with the Stafford and Leinster Squadrons I.Y., left camp at 6 a.m., crossed the spruit, and occupied the high ground on the far side. We could see some large parties of Boers hovering about just out of rifle shot, but beyond a little sniping, they made no attack.

About 2 p.m. we were relieved by the Infantry. At the same hour, the first wagon crossed the drift, but as repairs were frequently necessary, the crossing of the convoy was a terribly tedious business, and occupied the whole of that night and the following day (30 hours).

March 14th, the squadron left camp at 6 a.m., half squadron forming the advance guard, and half squadron, under Lieut. Twist, forming the right rear guard. To protect the convoy the latter had to occupy a ledge of rock, which they had great difficulty in holding, as only a very few men were available; and, after being under a very hot fire for nearly an hour, Sergt. W. Mahon was shot through the head, and died the following day. This half squadron, who, by this time, were heavily engaged by between 200 and 300 Boers, then retired under cover of the guns which had been sent to their assistance, and occupied a grassy slope, with practically no cover for men or horses. Here they had a very warm time, but escaped with only one casualty, No. 4861 Pte. McSweeney, wounded in the arm. It now became necessary to send Sergt. Maguire and ten men to hold a hill that ought to have been held by the Gloucester Yeomanry. Just as he was getting into position three volleys rang out, and No. 4820 Pte. Parr fell badly wounded through the thigh. On investigation this was found to be due to the negligence of a sergeant in charge of a flank guard post of the Gloucester Yeomanry, who were evidently in a very excited state, and were firing at anything.

Captain Wiggin, with the half-squadron forming the advance guard, received orders to cross the Klip River at De Lange's Drift, and occupy the high ground on the northern side. Brushing away a few snipers, he arrived at the river, which was found to be in flood, and the drift quite impassable. The column, therefore, camped on the southern side.

March 15th—22nd, as the river fell so slowly it was found necessary to float across all the wagons, about 300, and to ferry all the baggage over on a raft. All the horses and cattle were swum over, but it was not until the 22nd that the column marched into Standerton.

March 24th, the squadron paraded at 10 a.m., and together with two companies of Infantry, two guns, and a pom-pom, the whole under Colonel Colville, made a night march to Palmietkuil, 16 miles northeast. Boers had been reported to be sleeping at a farm near that place, we therefore rushed it at daylight, but found absolutely nothing.

March 25th, a day's rest at Palmietkuil.

March 26th, the squadron with the pom-pom started at 8 a.m., to reconnoitre. After being out about two hours we found about 30 Boers holding a ridge. We attacked them vigorously, and drove them off, wounding two, and capturing their small laagar, with all their blankets, and dinners ready for cooking. The Boers belonged to a small commando under Corporal Charlie Parsons. On the way back to camp Parsons worried the rear guard, and we were somewhat severely sniped by a party under Hans Nagle, which had come up from New Denmark. No. 4846 Pte. Letts was wounded in the wrist.

About 10.30 that night we were awoke by heavy firing at the outposts, and the whole force turned out, and lay down around the camp, but the alarm proved to be a false one, as the outposts had been firing at our Kaffir scouts, fortunately without hitting anyone.

March 27th, a very misty morning. About 8.30 a.m. we heard firing, and bullets began to drop into the camp, one gunner being wounded. We sent a hail of lead into the fog, and the sniping ceased. The mist cleared about 10 a.m., and the force marched over the railway crossing near Waterval. We destroyed a large quantity of forage, and captured some horses, and camped at Vlaklaagte.

March 28th, information was received that de Wet was about to attempt to cross the line from the south, and the force was ordered to take up a line of outposts from the Greylingstad mine on the right, to the Waterval River on the left, and a column under Col. Borroughs, R.A., came out from Standerton to take up the line from the Waterval River to Poortjie (110) on the Vaal. Colonel Colville's Column orders were that the squadron (who were reinforced by Lieut. Church's troop of A Squadron) was to form the advanced outpost line, watching the drift over the Water Vaal, and those over the Groot Spruit, whilst the Infantry and guns bivouacked in rear of the centre, at Volgestruisfontein (138). The Squadron took up its position just before nightfall, and remained watching that line until the morning of the 30th. Seldom had we spent two more unpleasant nights. The front was over six miles, which necessitated practically every man being utilized as vedettes. No Boers were seen, but we were attacked in great force by a commando of mosquitoes, and suffered severely.

During the night of the 28th, No. 3548 Corpl. Gavin was sent from Lieut. Church's picquet with a message to Colonel Colville. He was challenged by the Infantry sentry, and replied, but presumably did not make himself heard, as the Infantry outpost gave him a volley, which killed his horse, and wounded him in the arm.

March 30th, shortly after daylight the outpost line was drawn in, and the column concentrated. The whole force marched at 5.30 a.m., and crossed the Waterval, being sniped on the way by parties of Boers of Buys' Commando. The force halted for breakfast at Vaalbank (151) when it was joined by 70 J.M.R.'s and 100 Mounted Infantry, under Captain Ionides. During the halt information was brought in by Kaffirs that there was a commando of Boers with wagons just the other side of the Vaal at Roberts' Drift. We therefore mounted, and made a dash for the kopjes overlooking the drift. From there we could see the Boers, who had evidently got news of our proximity, streaming away south-west, but as they were already about two-and-a-half miles away, Colonel Colville did not consider it worth while to pursue, though the guns sent three or four shells into them. The J.M.R.'s crossed the river and captured some cattle. They had one man wounded by a few snipers who had lagged behind the main body. We camped that night under the kopje near the drift.

March 31st, at 9.30 a.m., the baggage arrived, escorted by another squadron of J.M.R.'s, which had picked it up at Vaalbank after our departure.

At 2 p.m. the squadron received orders to march at once to Waterval, which was reached at 6 p.m.

We had been cautioned that an attack might be expected by a party of Boers from Plat Kop (105). A few of them hung on our flank, but contented themselves, however, with a little sniping.

April 1st, marched at 8.30 a.m., and reached Standerton at 2.30 p.m., leaving behind Lieut. Church and his troop.

On arrival at Standerton, we found a big draft from England awaiting us. The share of the squadron was two officers, 2nd Lieuts. Lambert and Elliott, and 105 N.C.O.'s and men.

April 3rd, Captain Wiggin received orders to proceed with his squadron, to Katbosch, where he was reinforced by one company East Surrey, and one gun (15 pr.). With this force he was to watch De Lange's Drift, and other passages across the Klip River, and to cover the construction of blockhouses at Erdzak and Darling.

April 4th, on the following day this force moved to Katdoorn Krall (315), and took up a position so as to watch all the approaches from the Klip River, from Wildebeestkrall (83), and Kromdrai Station.

April 5th, half the squadron reconnoitred to the north of the railway, towards Diepspruit (81), and on the 6th and 7th reconnaisances were made, but very few Boers were seen.

April 8th, the force marched at 8.30 a.m., and returned to Standerton.

On 3rd April a big draft of 5 officers and 305 N.C.O.'s and men arrived from England, and were distributed among squadrons as follows:—

A Squadron, Lieut. J. T. Wigan, 99 N.C.O.'s and men.

B Squadron, 2nd Lieuts. Lambert and Elliott, 105 N.C.O.'s and men.

C Squadron, 2nd Lieuts. Kennard and Halswell, 101 N.C.O.'s and men.

Colonel Blagrove had been down to Newcastle, and had selected nearly 200 remounts, which came up with the draft, so now the Regiment was just under 700 strong at the front. There were daily drills for some of this draft, and the remounts, and also musketry.

On the 9th, 70 men under Captain Tremayne, with Lieut. Spencer, 2nd Lieuts. Halswelle and Kennard left Heidelberg at 10.30 p.m. for the Nigel mines.

The next day a reconnaisance was made towards Springs, and only two Boers were seen.

A party of Mounted Infantry came out during the day, and on the 11th a reconnaisance was made towards Langzeekoegat. A much superior force of Boers came on, and tried to get round the flanks of the squadron, which retired on the mines, the Boers following them up almost to within rifle shot of the infantry posts. During the retirement six of the mounted infantry got a long way away to the right, and were taken prisoners. No. 3781 Lance-Corpl Hedley was slightly wounded in the foot. Sergt. Priddle took a man whose horse had been shot behind him, and his horse bucked them both off, dislocating his shoulder. Six horses were wounded, and one killed. This party returned to Heidelberg the next day.

SOUTH AFRICAN WAR.   93

On the 10th, A Squadron joined Col. Colville's mobile column at Vlaklaagte. Lieut. Wigan remained at Greylingstad in charge of details of the squadron.

On the 10th, B Squadron relieved A Squadron at Greylingstad and Waterval. Capt. Wiggin and 2nd Lieut. Lambert went to Greylingstad, and Lieuts. Twist and Gubbins to Waterval. Lieut. Pepys stayed at Standerton, in charge of B Squadron details.

On the 11th, the mobile column marched for Witpoort at 8.30 a.m., A Squadron finding the advance guard, and the J.M.R.'s the rear guard. The J.M.R.'s, who were new at the game, instead of retiring, and fighting a rear-guard action, advanced and became involved seriously, and A Squadron had to go back and help them out.

April 14th, the mobile column marched to Uitkyk, near Frischgevaad.

On April 14th, General Clements took over command of the Standerton District, and General Wynne went to the Cape to take command there.

April 17th, A Squadron made a reconnaisance to the the east, and came in contact with the Boer picquets, which were driven in.

April 18th, Lieut. Denny and 2nd Lieut. Kennard and 72 men were sent out to the Nigel from Heidelberg.

April 19th, Lieut. Church was sent in from the mobile column at Uitkyk, with enteric. He went to hospital in Johannesburg, and was subsequently sent down to the convalescent depot at Mooi River, where he did duty, and returned to the Regiment on December 24th.

2nd Lieut. Cosens took Lieut. Church's place in A Squadron.

Lieut. Elliott went to hospital, and rejoined on May 11th.

Captain Wiggin was appointed to command a battalion of Mounted Infantry, with the local rank major, and left Greylingstad to take up his command at Standerton. That he commanded his battalion with success, is show by Lord Kitchener's despatch of August 8th, 1901, where his name is specially mentioned "for skilful and dashing leading of his Corps of Mounted Infantry," and in the final honour list he was promoted Brevet Lieut.-Colonel.

Captain Battye took over command of B Squadron.

April 28th, 2nd Lieut. Halswelle went to hospital. He was subsequently invalided home, and did not rejoin the Regiment in South Africa.

Lieut. Pepys with B Squadron details, left Standerton, to rejoin the squadron at Waterval and Greylingstad.

April 29th, the mobile column left the camp at Uitkyk at 4 a.m., to attack Hans Botha's laager at Langzeekogat. A Squadron was in advance, with the J.M.R.'s and guns in support.

It was, unfortunately, a very foggy morning. About 5.30 a.m. the fog lifted slightly, and Lieut. Stern (leading troop) sent out a section as far in advance as the mist would permit with safety. Shortly before

6 a.m., Guide Ward, who had been with the advance section, came galloping back, and told Lieut. Stern that he was just on the laager. The fog was now getting worse instead of better. The leading section (Corpl. Cave) on coming on the Boers' outpost, charged them, and Lieut. Stern's troop rushed the laager. Unfortunately, at this time we carried our rifles on the off side, making the use of the sword a matter of difficulty, and consequently this charge was not so effective as it would have been had the rifles been carried on the near side, as was done later.

The supporting troops were stopped by wire, and dared not fire, as it was impossible to distinguish friend from foe, and the Boers, got off, leaving four prisoners behind, all their wagons, blankets, food, etc., and many saddles.

No. 4290 Pte. Mills was shot through the heart, galloping into the laager, and No. 4281 Pte. Hayes, and No. 3880 Pte. Basden were at the same time mortally wounded. No. 4296 Lance-Corpl. House was slightly wounded through the thigh, and had eight bullets in his horse. Four horses were killed, including Lieut. Stern's, which was hit in five places, and six were wounded.

Later in the day, when the force was retiring to camp No. 3791, Pte. Holland, who was one of the rear guard, was most unfortunately hit by one of our shells, and killed.

Had it not been for the fog this squadron would have undoubtedly reduced Hans Botha's commando considerably.

Three Jews were found in a store close by, they behaved in a most disgusting manner, jeering at our wounded as they were brought in, and the store, in which there was a lot of ammunition, was burnt.

The same day, a patrol proceeding from Greylingstad, was surprised, and No 4773 Pte. Bakewell, was killed, and 4049 Pte. Prince and No. 4404 Pte. Capper, were wounded.

No. 4533 Pte. Burbridge was grazed by a bullet, but kept on firing, and hit three Boers before being captured.

May 2nd, Lieut. Pepys and 30 men of B Squadron joined the mobile column from Standerton, and formed a composite squadron, under Lieut. Denny, who joined with his party from the Nigel.

The column marched to Van Kolders. There were a good many Boers about, but except for some sniping from Klein Van Kolder the column was not molested.

May 3rd, Lieut. and Qr.-Master Rupert rejoined at Heidelberg from England.

The column marched to Smith's Drift. In the middle of the day, the rear guard had a sharp rear-guard action, the Boers coming up under cover of a grass fire.

May 4th, the column marched about 20 miles to Welgedacht.

The 2nd Cavalry Brigade (Col. Knox), 10th Hussars and 12th Lancers, marched through Heidelberg, going south in the direction of the Vaal.

SOUTH AFRICAN WAR. 97

May 5th, the column marched at 4 a.m., in a thick fog, and surprised the Boer outposts at a farm near Neikerks Vlei. The Boers galloped off, leaving a considerable quantity of cattle. Later in the day some Boers were driven off, leaving a Maxim, and a lot more stock behind. Camped at Uitkyk (236). Orders were received that the Regiment would concentrate at Standerton about the end of the month.

May 6th, the squadron with the mobile column was employed in clearing the country in the vicinity of the camp.

On May 7th, the column moved to Rademeyer's Farm, near Standerton. Captain Ogilvy took his squadron out from Heidelberg towards Malan's Krall, in order to intercept any Boers breaking back from the columns operating by the Vaal, and returned after dark. He was similarly employed the next day, but saw no Boers. Lieut. Twist went down to Mooi River, where he did duty till September, 1902. He was employed as Adjutant of the Cavalry Depot, at Mooi River from May 24th to September 20th, 1902.

On May 9th the Column marched at 7 a.m., through Standerton, picking up a convoy for Elliott's columns, which they escorted to De Lange's Drift.

On May 11th, the squadrons with the mobile columns made a reconnaisance, and sighted two wagons, which they pursued and captured, the Boers escorting them running away.

The squadrons were soundly sheltered by De Lisle's Column, luckily without any effect. Lieut. Jenkins returned to duty from the convalescent depot, Mooi River.

On May 12th, Lieut. Wigan joined A Squadron with the mobile column. Two squadrons 5th Dragoon Guards, and Major Wiggin's M.I. joined the mobile column, and camp was shifted to the south side of the river

The idea was for the column to work up the left bank of the Klip River, keeping in touch with the column on the right.

On May 15th, marched at 7 a.m. for Zandspruit. The 5th Dragoon Guards were engaged. A large quantity of stock was captured.

On May 16th, marched at 6.30 a.m., and cleared the farms on the way to Rustgen, where the column camped. The Boers were reported to have retired south-east.

50 men, 13th Hussars, and 100 men, K.R.R.'s, went out from Heidelberg to Da Hoek—a hill on the north side of the Zuicherbosch River, opposite the German Mission Station, in order to cut off any Boers that might try to break back from the columns operating along the Vaal. However, no Boers were seen, and this party returned next evening.

On May 17th, the mobile column marched at 7 a.m., cleared Piet Uys' Farm, collecting a lot of cattle, and camped near Joubert's Farm.

On the 18th, Capt. Ogilvy went down country sick, and did not rejoin again.

On the 19th, Major Williams, with the squadron made up with B and C Squadron men, under Lieut. Denny, and one squadron 5th Dragoon Guards, under

Captain Kennard, made a reconnaisance to Quagger's Nek, and found 40 Boers in a good position on his right, who had been following up Bethune's rear. He attacked both flanks simultaneously, and the Boers retired to the south. The 5th Dragoon Guards had two men hit.

On May 20th, the mobile column returned to Piet Uys Farm, and found it occupied. The advanced guard (Lieut. Denny's composite squadron) was held till Lieut. Stern made a flank movemnt with A Squadron, when the Boers retired.

On the 21st, a lot of Boers were about all day. The M.I. took a very steep burning hill near Steek Store. The 5th Dragoon Guards charged a kopje, and had two men wounded. The Boers disputed every ridge. No. 4185 Pte. Hawkins was wounded during the day.

May 22nd, stated at 9 a.m. to attack a big hill, on the top of which there was reported to be a Boer laager. The A and Composite Squadrons and the M.I. were opposed by a considerable number of Boers, and No. 3898 Pte. Hanton was wounded. However, the A and Composite Squadrons occupied the Nek when the Boers retired, and two troops under Lieut. Pepys were sent round the hill, while the remainder pushed on. When the troops retired, the Boers came on, and pressed Lieut. Pepys somewhat heavily. He lost two horses, and was lucky not to have any casualties among the men. One Boer was picked up, and certainly more were hit.

On the 23rd, marched over Commando Spruit, and were slightly opposed by 80 Boers during the day.

On the 24th, marched back to De Lange's Drift,

bringing in 20,000 sheep and over 1,000 head of cattle.

C Squadron and Head Quarters trained down to Standerton from Heidelberg, and B Squadron came in from Greylingstad and Waterval, and on the 24th we got into camp under Standerton Kop.

On the 25th, the detachment with the mobile column marched in, and the Regiment was together again for the first time since May 7th, 1900.

Till the 29th, the time was employed in drawing equipment and refitting, etc., and when the column marched out on the 29th it was probably the strongest and most complete Regiment in South Africa.

The strength of the Regiment marching out of Standerton was:—

18 Officers, 1 warrant officer, 566 N.C.O.'s and men, 571 horses (including draft and pack).

Lieut. and Quarter Master Rupert remained at Standerton, with 116 N.C.O.'s and men, and 40 horses.

Captain Tremayne, whose period of employment as Adjutant would have expired on June 8th, took over command of C Squadron, and Lieut. E. W. Denny took over the duties of Adjutant.

The distribution of the Officers on leaving Standerton was as follows:—

Col. H. J. Blagrove, Commanding.
Major M. A. Close, 2nd in Command.
Lieut. E. W. Denny, Adjutant.
Lieut. and Quarter Master G. Rupert, Quarter Master.
Lieut. M. F. Foulds, R.A.M.C., Medical Officer.

SOUTH AFRICAN WAR. 101

Lieut. R. St. C. Houston, A.V.D., Veterinary Officer.

A Squadron: Maj. C. Williams, Lieut. H. J. J. Stern, Lieut. T. H. S. Marchant, Lieut. J. T. Wigan, 2nd Lieut. C. E. Jenkins, 2nd Lieut. T. E. Lambert.

B Squadron: Capt. L. R. S. Battye, Lieut. W. Pepys, 2nd Lieut. L. B. B. Gubbins, 2nd Lieut. C. Elliot.

C Squadron: Capt. J. H. Tremayne, Lieut. A. W. B. Spencer, Lieut. G. H. Hodgkinson, 2nd Lieut. F. W. U. Cosens, 2nd Lieut. W. A. Kennard.

The column consisted of:—

5th Dragoon Guards, Col. St. J. Gore, C.B.

13th Hussars, Col. H. J. Blagrove, C.B.

Section Q Battery, R.F.A., Capt. and Bt.-Major Farrell.

East Lancashire, Col. Wright, C.B.

1 pom-pom, Lieut. Marton.

The column was commanded by Brigadier-General Gilbert-Hamilton.

His staff was:—

Lieut. Jenkins, 7th D.G.'s, A.D.C.

Major E. S. Bulfin, D.A.A.G.

Major Heath, R.E., Intelligence Officer.

Capt. P. J. Probyn, R.A.M.C., Medical Officer.

Captain Silburn, A.P.M.

May 29th, the column marched at 7.30 a.m. to Jonkerspruit (167) getting into camp about 2 p.m. A few Boers were seen during the day, evidently watching the movements of the column.

On May 30th, marched at 6 a.m. to De Pan (139) near the Waterval River.

The A Squadron Scouts came on some Boers near the Waterval River, but after exchanging a few shots about 50 were seen retiring to the south west. During this march No. 4942 Pte. Smith, who was marching with the baggage, was drowned, owing to his horse slipping into a deep water hole, whilst watering. No. 3025 Saddler-Sergt. Swatton, No. 5144 Pte. Cannon, and No. 4108 Pte. Griffiths made gallant efforts to save Pte. Smith. Sergt. Swatton was in great danger of being dragged under himself

The Officer Commanding issued the following order on reaching camp:—

> "All ranks are warned that the greatest caution should be exercised in watering horses in the pans or deep water holes which are met with on the veldt, as these pans are often 20 to 25 feet deep, and the sides precipitous. If it is desired to water horses at such places men must invariably dismount.
>
> "The Commanding Officer greatly regrets that No. 4942 Pte. Smith lost his life this day through ignorance of the danger with which watering at such spots is attended.
>
> "In connection with the above sad incident the Officer Commanding considers that the gallant attempt to save Pte. Smith's life by Sergt. Swatton and Pte. Cannon and Pte. Griffiths is worthy of the highest praise."

May 31st, marched at 6 a.m., in a dense fog, and bitterly cold. The baggage under Col. Wright, with the Infantry, marched to Wilgefontein (268) while the mounted troops made a detour down to the Vaal. It had been reported that a few Boers with a considerable quantity of cattle, etc., were just over the river in the O.R.C., somewhere close to Zand Drift. About 8 a.m. the fog lifted, and shortly afterwards the advance guard of the 5th Dragoon Guards was stopped. C Squadron was sent in support, and lost a horse, but the Boers retired, making no serious opposition. The whole force then crossed the river, and the A and B Squadrons were sent on after the Boers, who had retired to a farm in the bend of the river. B Squadron had to advance across the open, and came under a heavy fire, having three men, No. 3734 Corpl. Harding, No. 4034 Pte. Weale, and No. 4618 Pte. Dewhurst hit, and a horse killed. The Boers, of whom there were about 100, galloped off on seeing A Squadron coming round their right. A Squadron went on till they got to the river near Zand Drift, when it was useless to go any further, as the enemy had a long start, and were split up into several small parties. When the guns, which had been left behind during this gallop, came up, they fired a few rounds, and though we got a considerable quantity of stock, the Boers got off.

The force recrossed the river and got into camp at Wilgefontein (268) about 4 p.m.

Brigadier-General G. Hamilton was pleased to express his appreciation of the spirit shown by the 13th Hussars on this day.

On June 1st, marched to Greylingstad, starting at 7 a.m., and arriving at 11 a.m. On arrival we found that the column was under orders to entrain at once to Krugersdorp. A Squadron entrained during the afternoon, and B left in two trains, leaving at 11 p.m., and 3 a.m.

June 2nd, C Squadron and Head Quarters left during the morning, and arrived at Krugersdorp during the night, and had to detrain at once and bivouac near the station. A high piercing wind, with a stinging frost, ensured early rising the following morning, when we got together into a camp just outside the town. We heard that Dixon's Column had had a severe fight in the neighbourhood, and had many casualties.

June 4th, all the rifle buckets and sword frogs were altered so as to carry the rifles on the near side, and swords on the off side. The Etonians of the column all dined together. Lieut. and Qr.-Master Rupert, with the details, arrived from Standerton. 2nd Lieut. Lambert went to hospital. He was subsequently invalided home, and did not come out to South Africa again.

June 5th, marched at 7 a.m., with a large convoy for Naauport (214). Camped about 5 p.m. at Kaalfontein (105), a march of about 20 miles.

On June 6th marched to Zandfontein (256), halting in the middle of the day at Cyerfontein (22), about four miles from Naauport, and sending the convoy on.

The Brigadier got into communication with General Featherstonhaugh, and apparently we were not wanted, so the next day the column marched back to Cyerfontein, and took back the empty wagons from Naauport.

June 8th, marched to Kaalfontein. A force of 300 Boers were reported on our left, but none of them were seen, nor had any been seen since we left Krugersdorp.

On June 9th marched at 5.45 a.m. back towards Krugersdorp, and had a long outspan in the middle of the day, near the wood at Vlaklaagte, from where the wagons were sent into Krugersdorp, and we branched off to the west to Sterkfontein (70). When the advance guard (5th Dragoon Guards), arrived at Sterkfontein there was a considerable amount of sniping from the kopjes in the vicinity, and they had three men wounded. About 40 or 50 Boers were dodging about the hills, and kept on sniping till dark.

Lieut. A. W. Spencer went into Krugersdorp with the convoy, and was sent to hospital. He rejoined the Regiment again on July 16th.

June 10th, B Squadron and one squadron 5th Dragoon Guards left at 6 a.m. to escort our wagons out. They returned about noon, and then the column marched on about six miles to Dwarsvlei (60), below the Witwatersberg. The advance guard was sniped on the way by a few Boers, who quickly cleared, leaving a wagon loaded with oat forage.

On June 11th, Colonel Blagrove with B and C Squadrons, and one troop of A Squadron and the pompom detachment occupied Zeekoehoek (95) Pass. There was a certain amount of long range sniping during the day, but no casualties. Just below us was

Hartley's tobacco factory, with a large quantity of Magaliesberg tobacco. The machinery was all smashed up, and the building was afterwards burnt, as it was undoubtedly being used by the Boers.

The 5th Dragoon Guards, and the remainder of A Squadron occupied other passes, while Allenby's Column operated in the valley between the Witwatersberg and the Magaliesberg.

June 12th, remained at the same place. A company of Infantry arrived.

About the middle of the day, C Squadron, the strength of which at this time was 186 N.C.O.'s and Men, was ordered to proceed to Kaalfontein (105) to meet a convoy going to Naauport (214) from Krugersdorp. On arrival at Kaalfontein it was found that the convoy, which already had a strong escort of irregulars, had passed about two hours before, and it was after dark before the squadron came up to where the convoy was parked. This squadron escorted the convoy into Naauport the following day, and remained there till the 16th, when it rejoined the column, much to the annoyance of the officer commanding the convoy, who apparently wanted to keep the squadron as a permanency.

On June 13th, the Brigadier with the rest of the column came up.

June 14th, Colonel Blagrove, with A Squadron, and Captain Kennard's squadron, 5th Dragoon Guards, and some Infantry, was ordered to clear the Doornbosch Valley, a very fertile valley, which was laid absolutely waste. Families were brought in, and a large quantity of forage collected, and the rations were liberally supplemented, with fruit, chicken, etc. No one except perhaps the Boers, could complain that the work had not been thoroughly done.

B Squadron had left camp about 6 a.m., and marched through Zeehoehoek Pass to Allenby's Camp, and was then ordered to demonstrate against Damhoek Pass in the Magaliesberg. On retiring about 2.30 p.m., a few Boers sniped from the berg, and a horse was hit.

June 15th, B Squadron left Allenby's Column about 6 a.m., and rejoined the column just as it was starting to march to Cyerfontein (22).

June 16th, marched at 7.30 a.m. Colonel Blagrove, with two squadrons 13th Hussars, and the 5th Dragoon Guards, was sent to look for a force of Boers reported to be on our left. However, only twelve Boers were seen all day. Camped at Cyerfontein, not the same place as on the 15th.

June 17th, marched to Lilliefontein (334), and on June 18th marched to Tafel Kop, and remained there on the 19th.

June 20th, marched about 2 p.m. to Wet Pan, about eight miles on the way to Ventersdorp.

June 21st, marched to Ventersdorp.

June 22nd, marched to Klipfontein (530), seeing a few Boers, who kept a long way off.

June 23rd, marched at 7 a.m. Rawlinson's and Hickey's Columns close to us. Shortly after leaving camp a lot of cattle was seen on our left. Lieut. Cosens with his troop, was sent after these, and he did not return till late in the evening, bringing with him, however, a large herd of cattle. The column worked round by the Platberg, and got about six prisoners and some cattle.

The column camped at Reebokfontein (550), and Hickey's and Rawlinson's Columns camped near the same place.

We stayed at Reebokfontein, about six miles from Klerksdorp, till the 27th. On the 23rd, Lieut. and Qrmr. Rupert arrived at Klerksdorp from Krugersdorp.

On June 27th, about 9 a.m., the column marched from Reebokfontein, and halted for the day at the western end of Klerksdorp till 9.30 p.m., when we started for a night march on Hartbeestfontein, Allenby's and Weston's Columns co-operating.

On June 28th, at dawn, just short of Hartbeestfontein, we turned to the north, and watched the eastern side of the hills. We could hear the other two columns' musketry and pom-pom fire, but only saw about a dozen Boers. After it was considered that the hills had been cleared, we began to go back to Witpoort (620), and three engineeers were sent to blow up a farm under the hills.

Liebenberg and 30 of his men came down and captured them, and liberated them after taking their arms, etc. It appears that they were concealed in a kloof that Allenby's Column thought Hamilton's Column had searched, and vice versa.

However, it was annoying having these R.E. captured, and disappointing, inasmuch as three columns had made an uncomfortable and cold night march in hopes of capturing Liebenburg and his commando.

The result of this night march for all three columns was, one killed, two wounded, and seventeen unwounded Boers.

We bivouacked at Witpoort, where we arrived about noon.

Early in the morning Colonel Blagrove started off from camp for Klerksdorp to proceed home. There was not a man in the camp who was not genuinely sorry to say good-bye to their gallant Commanding Officer, and it was universally regretted that he had not been given an opportunity of leading a force against the Boers.

The Regiment turned out spontaneously to say goodbye, and to wish him what we all feel he deserves, the very best of good luck.

Colonel Blagrove, on leaving the Regiment, issued the following order:—

"The Colonel Commanding, on relinquishing command of the 13th Hussars, with whom he has served for over 26 years, desires to express his warmest thanks to the Officers, N.C.O.'s, and Men who have so loyally co-operated with him during his tenure of command.

"With their assistance, he is proud to think that he hands over the Regiment to his successor in as high a state of efficiency as it has ever been **before.**

"It is, at the present time, one of the strongest regiments in South Africa, and the experience gained by the Officers, N.C.O.'s, and Men during this long term of active service renders it second to none in every respect. The conduct of the N.C.O.'s and men of the regiment both in camp and in the field has been beyond praise, and will assuredly add to the reputation the Regiment has always borne.

"The best wish he can give to all ranks is a speedy and safe return home, and he hopes to be the first to welcome his old comrades when they land again in England."

Major M. A. Close now assumed command of the regiment.

During the night of June 29th—30th, some of the 5th Dragoon Guards made a night march in the hope of capturing Liebenberg, but were not successful, and rejoined the column in camp at Palmiefontein, about 10 miles along the Ventersdorp road.

July 1st, the "Gazette" of this date announced that Major W. C. Smithson was promoted Lieut.-Colonel to command the Regiment, vice Col. H. J. Blagrove, C.B., placed on half-pay, on completion of his period of service in command of the regiment. Captain Kenneth McLaren to be Major, vice W. C. Smithson promoted.

The column marched at 8 a.m. to Buffelsvlei (646) on the Schoon Spruit, passing Cronje's house. A number of farms were cleared, and families brought in.

SOUTH AFRICAN WAR.

July 2nd, marched at 8 a.m., leaving a squadron of the 5th Dragoon Guards concealed in the trees. A few Boers came down to look for ammunition after we marched, and this squadron got one wounded and two unwounded prisoners. Major Williams took A and C Squadrons out on the left flank and cleared several farms. Camped at Klipplaatz Drift, with Allenby's Column close to us. Lt. Stern, who had been seedy for the last day or two, was sent into Ventersdorp, where he developed enteric. He rejoined the Regiment on September 5th, at Olifant's Nek.

July 3rd, it took about four hours to get the column over the drift, and then marched south to Sterkstroom (130) about eight miles, and camped.

The Regiment, under Major Close, started at 6 a.m. for Kaffirskraal, and cleared the farms in that district, returning to camp at Rooiport (571).

The following telegram from Lord Kitchener was published:—

"The operations against the enemy not having yet resulted in teaching the Boers the uselessness of their struggle, it is necessary to exert renewed energy and vigour in bringing home to them the folly of continuing the war. The General Commanding in Chief feels confident that he can rely upon all ranks to exert every effort to obtain this object, and that all General Officers Commanding and commanders of troops in the field will actively use every means in their power to stamp out as rapidly as possible all armed resistance in their districts."

July 5th, the column marched to Ventersdorp. It was freely given out by the Intelligence boys before starting that there would be a night march; however, no orders were received for one till about 6 p.m., when C Squadron and a squadron of the 5th Dragoon Guards got their orders.

C Squadron started at 11 p.m., and before dawn surrounded Tweelingsfontein (606). At dawn the different parties advanced on the farm, and found some women and a loyal old man, who had four sons working for the British.

The 5th Dragoon Guards' squadron, who had been out to the east of the Ventersdorp-Potchefstroom road, and who had been none too well guided, saw a few Boers in the distance.

Both these squadrons joined the column at Witpoortje (567) and camped there.

July 7th, marched at 5.30 a.m. to Potchefstroom.

July 8th, a rest day.

July 9th, the Infantry and half squadron (Lieut. Jenkins) under Major Heneage, took a convoy into Ventersdorp.

The column marched to Rietkuil (537).

Captain Battye and Lieut. Cosens remained at Potchefstroom in charge of some young horses, and Lieut. Pepys took over command of B Squadron.

July 10th, marched to Lustfontein (281).

July 11th, Lieut. Pepys and 60 men of B Squadron turned out at 4.30 a.m. in hopes of surprising Boers in a farm, but they were not there. The farm was cleared, and the families brought in. Major Williams with 50 men was out all the morning clearing farms.

July 12th, marched to Witpoortje. Major Heneage's escort for the convoy rejoined.

C Squadron made a detour round by Bulskop (374), and Tweelingsfontein (606), and rejoined in the evening, with some cattle and sheep, having seen no Boers.

July 13th, marched back to Ventersdorp.

July 14th, marched to Sterkstroom on the Schoon Spruit. Lieut. Hodgkinson and the rear guard came in for some sniping.

July 15, marched at 1.30 p.m. to Palmietfontein, and moved off again at 10.30 p.m., Major Williams and his half squadron remaining behind to escort the ox convoy when it came up.

At daylight, C Squadron was sent on to Lamoenfontein (645), and found a Boer doctor and his assistant and two sick Boers. There were evident traces of Boers having been recently at the farm, and the doctor said that Smuts had been there, but had left the previous evening to take part in a raid into the Cape Colony.

B Squadron had surrounded another farm, but without finding any Boers. We bivouacked at Lamoenfontein, and the baggage arrived in the evening.

July 17th, rest day. The ox convoy arrived midday, and with it Lieut. Spencer, who was not better, and Lieut. Cosens with 60 horses.

July 18th, marched to Hartebeestfontein. There were a few Boers about, and one of them was captured.

Captain Battye and his party proceeded to Klerksdorp from Potchefstroom, and remained in command of the details.

July 19th, marched to Klerksdorp, and stayed there on the 20th. Lieut. Spencer went to hospital. He was subsequently invalided home, and rejoined the Regiment at Greylingstad in May, 1902.

July 21st, marched to Rhenoster Spruit (16).

July 22nd, the column marched to Klipfontein (2), and just before reaching camp the Boers opened fire on the rear guard, wounding two men of the 5th Dragoon Guards, and also No. 4065 Pte. Garrett, who was shot in the thigh, and knocked over, but kept on firing till hit again through both wrists.

B and C Squadrons started at 4.30 a.m., to clear the country on the right of the column.

Major Close, with B Squadron, collected some cattle and sheep, and a wagon, and took a prisoner after he had wounded the guide. A commando of 800 Boers was said to be about. C Squadron also collected some stock, and cleared several farms. The rear guard was fired on at long range most of the way back.

July 23rd, marched at 5.30 a.m. for Woolmaranstad. About noon Boers with cattle were reported to the east of the road in a very rough country. A Squadron, who were sent on in advance came under a heavy fire, two men being hit. No. 4536 Pte. Adams, and No. 4018 Pte. Frame, and also Guide Murphy. The Boers immediately retired through the hills, and after collecting much stock, the column camped near Woolmaranstad.

July 24th, remained at Woolmaranstad, and burned the town. Captain Clay, with a troop of 5th Dragoon Guards, was sent out to Leeuwfontein (137) and came in contact with about 100 Boers. Seven of his men were captured, and immediately released, after having been stripped of their clothes and boots.

July 25th, marched to Brandewynskuil (15) on the Makuasi Spruit. The Boers hung round the rear guard for the first two or three miles out of Woolmaranstad, but did no damage.

July 26th, marched at 1.30 a.m. by Dofferspruit (215) and at dawn surprised a Boer laager near Klipkuil (63). The 5th Dragoon Guards in front, galloped on, and the Boers fled to the hills. Potgeiter, the commandant, escaped in a Cape cart. We were kept back with the guns. The 5th Dragoon Guards had one man wounded, and three officers' horses hit. C Squadron had marched with the baggage through the night, and at dawn was sent on to block the drift over the Wolve Spruit at Rustfontein (475), picking up three prisoners on the way. The column reached Rustfontein about 1 p.m., and the baggage arrived two hours later.

The total captures were 10 prisoners, 23 wagons, a few horses, and a very large herd of cattle and sheep.

The following extract from Brigade Orders was published for information:—

"The Brigadier General Commanding congratulates the troops on the well earned success to-day.

"He fully appreciates the cheerful and ready manner which all ranks have shown in carrying out his orders on every occasion, and which has helped us so materially in to-day's success. The promptness and dash of the squadron 5th Dragoon Guards under Major Eustace especially calls for mention."

A few days later (August 1st) General Hamilton received the following wire from Lord Kitchener.

"This is very good. Please tell your troops I am much pleased, and shall hope to hear soon of further success."

July 27th, marched at noon to Cyfergat (69).

The rear guard (Lieut. Norwood, with 50 men. 5th Dragoon Guards) got left a long way behind bringing on the sheep, and the Boers, who were all dressed in khaki, bothered it a good bit. B Squadron was sent back to his assistance, and the Boers retired.

July 28th, rest day. The first Sunday we spent in camp since leaving Standerton.

July 29th, marched to Syferkuil (124) without seeing any Boers.

July 30th, marched back to our old camp at Rhenoster Spruit (16).

SOUTH AFRICAN WAR.   117

July 31st, marched back to Klerksdorp, where we stayed till August 5th.

August 2nd, a draft of 63 N.C.O.'s and men arrived, bringing the strength of the regiment, including details now at Klerksdorp, to 749 N.C.O.'s and men, and 519 horses.

The total strength of the Regiment in South Africa was 847 N.C.O.'s and men, 45 of whom were in various hospitals.

August 5th, marched at 8 a.m. for Buisfontein (186), and on arrival there information was received that some Boers had gone through the hills to Geduld (158). The mounted troops were pushed on rapidly through a narrow pass, with very steep sides. After getting about three quarters of the way through this pass about 40 Boers on the neck at the end opened a heavy fire on the advanced squadron (C) and stopped them. The Boers waited until the troops had got up the sides of the pass to work round their flanks, when they galloped off. The column then proceeded to Geduld, and the baggage did not get into camp till a very late hour.

August 6th, remained halted during the day.

August 7th, started at 12.30 a.m., and arrived at Kaffirs' Kraal (185) at dawn, and saw no sign of the enemy. After searching the hills in the vicinity, about 40 Boers were reported, and C Squadron had a long gallop after them, but could not get near them. Shortly afterwards more Boers were reported to our right, and A and B Squadrons, and one squadron of the 5th Dragoon Guards went after them, but after a long gallop the pursuit was given up as the Boers had too long a start. After a very long and tiring day for horses we camped at Nooitgedacht, the baggage getting there before us.

August 8th, halted for the day, but marched on.

August 9th at 2 a.m. The 5th Dragoon Guards crossed the Schoon Spruit at Mahamsvlei, and we crossed at Brakspruit, and made a combined movement round the Platberg to Goodgevonden, where we camped without having seen any Boers. Just as we were going into camp a Cape cart and some cattle were reported among the Platberg hills. Lieut Pepys, with half squadron, was sent after them, and after going through a nasty bit of country he caught them up, and captured four prisoners, 162 head of cattle, 300 sheep, 12 ponies, and a Cape cart.

August 10th, C Squadron left camp at 4 a.m., and made a detour by Bullskop without seeing any Boers, and joined the column about the middle of the day.

The column marched at 5.40 a.m., and collected a considerable quantity of stock. In the afternoon about 60 Boers were reported driving cattle away. Major Williams and half A Squadron were sent after them, and drove them off, capturing 180 head of cattle, and 300 sheep. Camped at Leeuwfontein (656).

August 11th, marched at 7 a.m. for Elandskuil (110) near Ventersdorp.

August 12th, marched at noon to Ventersdraai (28) about three miles the other side of Ventersdorp, leaving the ox convoy at that place.

We started again at 10.30 p.m., and marched through the night to Klipkrantz (300) arriving about 7 a.m., and bivouacked for the day. During the night a wagon broke down, and Lieut. Jenkins and his troop got left behind, but caught us up about 8 a.m.

August 13th, marched again at 3.30 p.m. to Leeuwfontein (496), arriving there at 9 p.m., and camped for the night.

August 14th, started at 3 a.m. and marched to Koperfontein (650), where we encountered some Boers taking a prisoner and a lot of cattle and five wagons. Allenby's column, earlier in the morning, had engaged about 200 Boers, under Steynkamp, and had one officer of the Carabiniers killed (Lieut. Till), and had about six men wounded. We retired to Basfontein (923) about noon, and the baggage coming about the same time, got into camp.

On August 15th marched to Groenfontein, about 12 miles, capturing three Boers, with a wagon and some ammunition. B Squadron, on the right flank, were sniped pretty freely to start with, but had no casualties.

Halted on the 16th.

On 17th—18th, marched to Klipkrantz (300) and the following day into Ventersdorp.

On the 19th, a short march to Modderfontein (642). The 5th Dragoon Guards, 100 Infantry, and two guns left us to go to Naauwpoort (214) to take a convoy to Rustenberg.

On 20th, marched to Witkopje (103), on the Mooi River.

On the 21st, marched to Welverdiend, on the Potchefstroom Krugersdorp line. Lieut.-Col. Smithson rejoined, and took over command of the regiment. It was a year all but a day since he had been wounded, and we were all very glad to see that he had so completely recovered, and that he had had the good fortune to get command of the regiment.

Major Close left us from here, on leave, pending retirement, and very sorry we all were to say good-bye to him.

On October 4th, Major Close was placed on retired pay.

On 22nd, marched at 2.30 p.m. to Wonderfontein (653).

On the 23rd, marched to Holfontein.

Lieut. Pepys and 70 men of B Squadron escorted the section of Q Battery, R.F.A., to Kaalfontein (105), who were going into Krugersdorp. Their place on the column was taken by two guns 66th Battery. The 5th Dragoon Guards were at Kaalfontein on their way to Naauwpoort.

On 24th started at 6 a.m. Long march to Bufflesfontein (387) under Naauwpoort. Lieut. Pepys joined us en route, and the 5th Dragoon Guards rejoined in the evening.

On 25th, marched at 6 a.m., with a large convoy to Ollivant's Nek. The last wagon did not get in till about 7 p.m.

Captain Fish, A.P.M., went out foraging with the Provosts, and managed to get himself and No. 3408 Pte. Pritchard hit.

On 26th, Lieut.-Col. Smithson, with 200 men 13th Hussars, started at 2 a.m., and at dawn about half a dozen Boers were seen, but a long way off. The kloofs were thoroughly searched, and five wagons and a quantity of food stuff were burnt.

One Boer was captured.

The 5th Dragoon Guards took the convoy on to Rustenburg, returning the next day.

On 27th, orders were received to form a Special Service Squadron, to be composed of picked men and horses. 75 men were to be selected from the 13th Hussars, and 25 from the 5th Dragoon Guards, to be under the command of Captain Kennard, 5th Dragoon Guards, who was to have with him Lieuts. Wigan and Elliott, 13th Hussars, and Lieut. Dunbar, 5th Dragoon Guards. This squadron never did anything, however.

On 28th, escorted the empty convoy back to Naauwpoort, and camped at Buffelsfontein again.

On the 29th, the column was split up into different parties to prevent he enemy breaking through anywhere between the Magaliesberg and Naauwpoort. The 5th Dragoon Guards were on the right, B Squadron at Ollivant's Hook, then A Squadron, then C Squadron, and the Infantry on the left.

Other columns were working down from the west and north-west.

B Squadron caught eight Boers hiding in a kloof in the morning.

We remained in these positions till the morning of September 1st without seeing a Boer.

On September 1st, the column moved from the position it had been holding for the last three days, and marched to Duikerbuilt (962). A very rough country, with many kloofs to be searched.

On 2nd September, marched to Doornfontein. Captain Stewart, 5th Dragoon Guards, captured four Boers and one wagon.

On 3rd September, heavy firing by our outposts during the night. Sergt. Winter reported that a party of Boers had ridden up to his post. The next morning three dead ponies with saddles were found. We marched to Roodeval (952), picking up 10 prisoners, who were hiding in the bush in different places, and encamped near Kekewich's Column. We heard that the Boers, whom we were supposed to block between Naauwpoort and the Magaliesberg, had broken away to the north-west.

On September 4th, marched back to Ollifant's Nek, picking up eight Boers hiding in the bush. B Squadron made a wide detour on our right, and brought in a prisoner and a lot of cattle.

On September 5th, Lieut Stern with 55 men and 52 horses, joined the column. The prisoners and captured stock were sent into Rustenberg.

September 6th, marched to Kopperfontein (650), and camped close to Kekewich's Column.

On 7th, marched to Dwarsfontein.

On 8th, marched to Klipkrantz (300).

On 9th, marched to Vetersdorp.

On 10th marched at 5 a.m. along the Litchenberg road to Wildfontein (123). Two troops of C Squadron and B Squadron went on in hopes of catching De la Rey, but only found eight most persistent snipers, and got back to camp about 4 p.m.

On 11th marched at 7 a.m., the camp to be at Syferkuil (42). Each squadron was to act more or less independently as long as touch was kept with the main body. A few prisoners and a lot of cattle were captured by the time we got to Kaffirs' Kraal (185), when the Regiment was concentrated, and Lieut.-Col. Smithson took us on to Lamoenfontein (645).

B Squadron, in advance, came under a warm fire on approaching the farm, but galloped on, and took eight prisoners.

The other two squadrons prevented a mob of ponies being driven off, and brought in some wagons and cattle. We got back to camp after dark.

The Brigadier-General Commanding sent the following communication to the Officer Commanding :—

"I should like you to let your Regiment know that I consider that all ranks have worked with great efficiency and zeal during the last 34 hours. The captures during the last two days are chiefly owing to the exertions of your Regiment, and your capture of 120 remounts from the Boers is important. I hope you will express the appreciation of the good work done by your Regiment to all ranks."

The total of the captures for the last two days was 25 prisoners, 120 ponies, 450 cattle, 600 sheep.

September 12th, halted at Syferkuil (42).

On September 13th, marched at 7 a.m. to Witpoort (62) on the Schoon Spruit.

On September 14th, marched at midnight 13th—14th to the Elandslagte (598) Gold Mines, without success, and returned to Klerksdorp. When the Regiment arrived at Klerksdorp, we heard that the enemy had been particularly active in the vicinity, and had made repeated attacks on the cattle guards, which had to be strengthened by men from the details.

On the 7th, one of the posts was attacked by the Boers in considerable numbers, and No. 2711 Pte. Smith was killed, and his body was mutilated in a most barbarous manner.

The Patriotic Fund granted Pte. Smith's widow a pension of 5s. a week, and 1s. 6d. a week for each child.

The following day the cattle guards were again seriously attacked, and No. 3981 Pte. Mackie was killed, No. 3592 Pte. Tanner went back under a heavy fire to assist a comrade (whose horse had become restive), to mount, and while doing so was mortally wounded, and died in a few hours. For this gallant action he was mentioned in despatches. No. 4821 Pte. Mallard was also severely wounded, having both bones of his leg broken.

The Boers refused to give him any water, though they had plenty, and could get plenty. This man was stripped, and remained out in the intense cold all night, and could not be found by the ambulance until the following day.

On September 18th, a party of 60 men taken from the three squadrons, with Captain Tremayne, Lieuts. Stern and Elliot, marched about midnight 17th—18th, by the Buffelsdorn Goldmines, so as to come down on a farm at Goodevonden (377), and drive some Boers that were known to be about there into the Platberg. Captain Kennard, 5th Dragoon Guards, and Captain Clay, 5th Dragoon Guards, marched the same night. Captain Clay posted his men among the different passes in the Platberg, and Captain Kennard marched so as to come down on Goodevonden by Doornfontein (340). At dawn we surprised about 20 or 30 Boers, who galloped off, leaving many blankets and some saddles behind. Lieut. Elliot pursued these Boers, and drove them into the Platberg, when unfortunately the 5th Dragoon Guards fired on him in the bad light. Captain Clay's party was not strong enough to thoroughly hold the country he had to watch, and the Boers broke through, leaving two wounded and three unwounded prisoners in our hands.

The Regiment remained at Klerksdorp till the 21st, when it trained down to Dundee. The East Lancashire left the column here, and on arrival at Dundee the West Kents, under Captain Moody, joined.

Louis Botha had concentrated a large force, with the intention of invading Natal, and in order to frustrate this, several columns went down to the Natal border.

One of the trains conveying the 5th Dragoon Guards ran off he line near Zandspruit. Four men were injured, and several horses had to be destroyed. This caused much delay to the trains coming behind, and though the first party left Klerksdorp early on the morning of the 21st, it was not till the evening of the 24th that the Regiment got together again at Dundee.

On the 23rd, the details, under Captain Battye, trained down to Dundee. Lieut. and Qrmr. Rupert remained at Klerksdorp with the heavy baggage.

On September 24th, Major Williams assumed the duties of acting Second in Command, and Lieut. H. J. J. Stern took over the command of A Squadron.

September 25th, marched to de Jager's Drift, where Pulteney's Column and the J.M.R.s, under Colonel Stewart, were encamped. Some of the wagons did not get in till after midnight. We soon found that getting the transport along in this part of the country was very different to where we had come from. The veldt so soft that the wagons were continually sinking in up to the axles, and when we got into the Vryheid district the hills were appalling.

On September 26th, crossed the Buffalo River, and camped on the other side next to a squadron of the 8th Hussars.

General Clements was in command of the various columns in these operations.

On September 27th, Pulteney's Column went off to join General Bruce Hamilton in Zululand. Our column and the J.M.R.s marched to Rooi Kop, on the way to Vryheid.

We heard reports that Boers had attacked posts in Zululand, but it was not very clear what had happened. The summary of news received on the 29th contained the following:—

"Major Chapman with a small force in charge of a post in Zululand, made a successful defence on the 26th inst. against 1500 of the enemy under Louis Botha. The enemy admit a loss of 19 killed, but natives say that they were carrying away their dead and wounded all day on the 27th inst.

On September 28th, the Regiment and about 400 J.M.R.s, started at 5.30 a.m., and marched to Scheeper's Nek, escorting a convoy which went on into Vryheid, and waited on the Nek till it returned in the afternoon, and escorted it back to Rooi Kop.

On September 29th, marched south, and crossed the Blood River, near Vechkop (68) or Dingaan's Hill, where the Boers finally defeated Dingaan.

A very bad drift to finish up with, and after the lines were got down strong fatigue parties had to be told off to assist the wagons across, the last wagon getting in about 10 p.m.

On Sepember 30th, the J.M.R.s marched back to De Jager's Drift, for convoy work.

Our column marched on to Vant's Drift, the 5th Dragoon Guards going on to Rorke's Drift. We started at 6 a.m., and did not get the last of the baggage in till 9 p.m.

October 1st, Major Williams, with 80 men of B Squadron, marched at 8 a.m. to hold Zietman's Drift, and was joined the next day by a squadron of the 5th Dragoon Guards.

On October 3rd, Major Williams and the B Squadron party at Zeitman's Drift, returned to Vant's Drift after dark.

During the last three days 11 horses died from eating tulip grass.

On October 4th, the J.M.R.s remained to watch the drifts, and our column marched to Nondweni.

On October 5th, marched to Spitz Kop (495), and the following day to Bethel (683), crossing the White Umvelosi River.

On October 5th, Captain Battye proceeded with all available horses and men to De Jager's Drift, and the same evening escorted a convoy to Rooi Kop. This party remained at Rooi Kop for eight days, doing constant escorts to convoys to and from Scheeper's Nek.

On October 7th, Major Williams, with 80 men of A and 80 men of B, escorted 120 wagons to Vryheid to fill up, and returned on the 9th. 100 men of C Squadron went out about five miles, up a very steep and high hill, in order to get helio communication with Vryheid. It was a very misty day, and only three messages were got through all day.

During the last two days, General Walter Kitchener had been having severe fighting in the Schurweberg, with what was evidently General Louis Botha's rear guard, so, though his intended raid on Natal had proved abortive, he had got back, and we were too late to cut him off.

On October 10th marched to Brakfontein (352).

Major Heath, R.E., Intelligence Officer, with Lieuts. Hodgkinson and Cosens, and 50 men, and 50 men of the 5th Dragoon Guards, started at midnight, and at daylight surprised about a dozen Boers, and captured four.

On October 11th, marched at 5.30 a.m., and marched to Vryheid, where we had a long outspan, and in the afternoon went on, and camped at Scheeper's Nek.

On October 12th, marched to Rooi Kop, from where General Clements went into Newcastle. 22 N.C.O.'s and men, part of a draft that had arrived from England joined the Regiment. The remainder of this draft (22 N.C.O.'s and men) joined the Regiment on November 6th, at Pretoria.

On October 13th, marched to Waaihoek. Lieut. Hodgkinson and 70 men remained at Rooi Kop to escort convoys, and Captain Battye's party returned to Dundee.

October 14th, marched at 5.30 a.m., to Twfelfontein (160) (Knight's Farm) having a long halt just outside Utrecht before climbing up that awfully steep and long hill.

Here we heard that the Distinguished Service Order had been conferred on Lieut.-Col. Smithson, Major McLaren, Major Ogilvy, and Captain Taylor, and that Captain (Local Major) Wiggin had got a brevet majority.

On October 15th, marched to Elan's Nek (4) came upon a few Boers with cattle, and rumour had it that the Boers were about in considerable numbers.

It seemed just the sort of country they would like.

Plumer, Campbell, Pulteney, Colville, and Garratt's Columns, besides ourselves, were all co-operating.

On October 16th, the camps remained standing, but all the troops went out searching kloofs, and found several small laagers, with women and wagons.

On October 17th, marched at 7 a.m. to Schikhoek (24) over the Chakka Spruit, a very hilly trek. After getting into camp, the Regiment with a gun turned out as quickly as possible to help Pulteney's Column, which was being stopped by the Boers on our left. He, however, did not require our assistance, and after our own gun had had a couple of practice rounds at our advance scouts, and having got communication with the other column, we returned to camp, getting in about 8 p.m.

On October 18th, the weather was too misty to admit of anything being done.

Marched to Tambookesbult (32).

On October 19th, operations still suspended owing to thick weather.

On October 20th, it is hard to give an intelligible account of this day's doings.

Orders and counter orders came with such lightning rapidity that no one had time to think at the time, nor does the result throw much light on what the idea

was. We marched about 6.30 a.m., leaving the
camp standing, with the intention, it was supposed,
of clearing the bush and hills. This idea was abandoned, and we marched to Luneberg Mission Station,
and the baggage was ordered to join us there. When
the baggage arrived we were ordered to get out our
cloaks, waterproof sheets, rations, and forage, for three
day. Having packed these on our horses we went at
a very rapid rate for about five miles over a rough
and hilly country, and sat down and waited for our
baggage, when we pitched camp. The baggage arrived
shortly after 5 p.m., and we then learnt that the
operations during the next few days would take place
over a country impassable for wagons, so that packs
for the mules must be made out of sacks, to carry
forage and rations for three days. Several methods
were tried, but very few of the mules seemed to
enter into the spirit of the thing, and just when we
had come to the conclusion that we should probably
have to do without forage and rations, an order came
that our experiments were unnecessary.

On October 21st, marched to Groethoek (250) with
our baggage.

A Squadron and the 5th Dragoon Guards cleared a
good extent of bush. One man was hit.

Campbell's Column, on our right, recaptured two of
Gough's guns that were taken on September 17th near
Scheeper's Nek. Guide Ahn was killed while out with
the J.M.R.s.

The camp moved to Paardeplaats (21).

On October 22nd, a very wet morning. The convoy returned to Luneberg. C Squadron, with one squadron 5th Dragoon Guards, under Colonel Gore, occupied the hills overlooking the basin to the west, from where we could see the blockhouses along the Pietretief road. Short rations for man and horse.

On October 23rd, A and B Squadron, and two squadrons 5th Dragoon Guards, and the Infantry, searched the basin, bringing in a lot of cattle, ponies, and saddles. One man of the 5th Dragoon Guards was wounded. The rations were all but out.

On October 24th, the convoy returned with one day's rations. C Squadron rejoined the Regiment, and camp was moved back to La Belle Esperance.

A Squadron was out all day, but had not come across any Boers.

On October 25th, camped at Shickhoek (24).

On October 26th, marched to Eland's Nek.

Lieut. Stern, with his squadron (A) was sent off to help the J.M.R.s through Pivaan's Poort, and did not rejoin the Regiment till early next morning.

No. 3050 Corpl. W. H. Campbell, who came out with a draft in March, 1900, but went from Mooi River before rejoining the Regiment to the S.A.L.H., in which corps he held the rank of sergeant, died of wounds received in action at Witbank, Orange River Colony.

This N.C.O. was mentioned in Lord Kitchener's despatch of June 23rd, 1902.

On October 27th, marched at 5.30 a.m., and after proceeding a short distance, it was reported that some Australians were being stopped in Zackeuil's Nek, so the column branched off to the right, and after shelling the Nek marched on to Wonderhoogte. The final hill looked impossible for the baggage. However, it was got up eventually.

On October 28th, marched at 5.30 a.m., to Wakerstroom.

Lieut. M. F. Foulds, R.A.M.C., went to hospital.

On October 29th, marched to Volksrust.

On October 30th, entrained for Standerton.

The transport had to entrain from Charlestown, and did not get in till the next day.

We encamped near the detail camp.

On October 17th, the details trained to Newcastle, where Lieut. Hodgkinson and his party joined them from Rooi Kop on the 22nd.

On the 23rd, the details and Lieut. Hodgkinson's party marched by easy stages to Volksrust, arriving on the 26th, and were then ordered to proceed to Standerton. Captain Battye, with about 40 of the worst horses, trained up to Standerton, arriving on the 27th.

Lieut. and Qrmr. Rupert, who had remained at Klerksdorp, arrived at Standerton on the 27th, with a lot of necessary stores to refit the Regiment.

Lieut. Hodgkinson marched the remainder of the

details from Volksrust to Standerton, and arrived on the 30th.

The night of October 30th—31st, was a very wild night, with floods of rain. The next morning we began to get things a bit straight, and generally refit, when an order came in the middle of the day that we were to march during the afternoon.

News had been received that Benson's Column had been very severely handled, but no details were known or made public. At 4 p.m. Brigadier-General Hamilton, with our column, commanded by Col. Gore, 5th Dragoon Guards, Allenby's Column, and De Lisle's Column, marched at 4 p.m. to New Denmark (33) ,and halted till 11 p.m., and then marched on through the night to Trichaardsfontein (91). There were a lot of Boers about, and B Squadron had 3963 Pte. White, and 4836 Corpl. Mumford hit. The former died of his wounds the same night. Civil-Surgeon Harding, who went out to look after Pte. White, was wounded, but as he only had a brassard on his arm, and no red cross flag, the Boers could not possibly distinguish that he was a medical officer.

A man of the Carabiniers was killed.

Communication was established with Benson's Column, who had been relieved by Barter's Column from Springs. They did not want any further assistance, and were going into the line at Brug Spruit.

The baggage of the different columns, under Major Williams, left Standerton about 7 p.m., and marched till 2 a.m.. and then outspanned till 6 a.m.

Throughout the day they had Boers hovering round, and at one time about 300 made a faint-hearted attack, which was not of a serious nature.

However, 4368 Pte. Musgrave, and No. 3531 Sergt. Lloyd, of the rear guard, were both wounded.

The former was knocked off his horse, and was unable to remount, and Sergt. Lloyd, though wounded in the foot, gallantly went back under a heavy fire, and brought in his wounded comrade.

Regimental orders, 1st November, 1901, contained the following:—

"The Officer Commanding wishes to place on record the great gallantry displayed by Sergeant Lloyd, who, notwithstanding the fact that he was wounded at the time, returned in the face of a heavy fire, and brought in a wounded comrade. Sergeant Lloyd was subsequently invalided home, and in July, 1902, was discharged from the service as medically unfit, receiving a temporary pension, which was increased by 6d. a day on account of 'Distinguished Conduct.'"

The wagons arrived about 4 p.m., and the three columns camped at Trichaardsfontein (91).

On November 2nd, halted at Trichaardsfontein.

November 3rd, returned to New Denmark in heavy rain.

November 4th, returned to Standerton. The last few miles in heavy rain.

A Squadron and Head Quarters entrained at 8 p.m., for Pretoria.

On November 5th, the remainder of the Regiment entrained for Pretoria, arriving the following morning, and went into camp just outside the town on the Erstefabriken road.

The Regiment remained at Pretoria till November 13th.

On the 7th, Lieut. and Qrmr. Rupert brought up the details from Standerton, and camped at Johnson's redoubt, just above our camp.

Captain Battye stayed at Standerton for some days to obtain remounts.

Civil-Surgeon G. T. White joined the Regiment for duty.

On November 9th, the following extract from W.O. letter of 9th October, was published for information :—

"Major C. Williams has been selected for the appointment of Second in Command of the 13th Hussars, vice Major M. A. Close, retired."

During the time we were at Pretoria there was daily a thunderstorm. On the 10th four men of the 5th Dragoon Guards were struck by lightning, and though no one was killed, they were all more or less severely injured.

On November 11th, the column paraded for the presentation of the D.S.O. to Major Heath, R.E., and Captain Probyn, R.A.M.C.

SOUTH AFRICAN WAR.   137

The following extract from the "Gazette" of October 15th, was published:—

"13th Hussars.—Captain A. H. R. Ogilvy, D.S.O., to be Major, vice Major M. A. Close, retired October 5th."

During the time we were at Pretoria, we were busy refitting in every respect.

We took over about 148 horses from the 5th Dragoon Guards.

On November 13th, the Regiment, 537 strong, two guns (Lieut. Mortimore) and Captain Morley, and 30 of his scouts, marched at 1 p.m., under Lieut.-Col. Smithson, D.S.O., to Erstefabricken, and camped near the distillery. At midnight, 13th—14th, C Squadron started to make a detour, in order to hold a line near Tweefontein (522), and the remainder marched at 4 a.m. No Boers were seen. We then marched through a very rough country with a lot of bush to Wagon Drift (453).

On November 15th, marched to Hartebeestspruit (286). Lieut. Marchant on the left took two prisoners. One of them, with a bandolier with some split bullets in it, after a little pressure, gave some useful information.

Lieut.-Col. Smithson decided on a night march, and started at 10.30 p.m., taking with him B Squadron, and half A Squadron, and half C Squadron (the country was too rough for the guns), and marched to Kameelpoort Nek (354), and on to Klopperdam—a very rough country, with thick bush, and rocky kopjes. A wide area was searched, but the Boers had cleared. Lieut.-Col. Smithson returned to camp, which had been moved back to Wagon Drift, at 5.30 p.m., destroying 45 sacks of mealies on the way.

On November 17th, marched back to Tweefontein. Half A Squadron, and half C Squadron, with Morley's Scouts, remained concealed in a wood near Wagon Drift during the day, and after dark made a night march on two farms, but found no Boers, and returned to Tweefontein just as the Regiment was moving off for Erstefabricken, where we camped.

On November 19th, returned to Pretoria, and remained there till December 5th.

Every evening there was a terrific thunderstorm, which flooded the camp out. This evening (November 19th), three horses of B Squadron and one of A Squadron were killed by lightning, and the tent in which S.Q.M.S. Page was, was struck, and the pole split to atoms. S.Q.M.S. Page was fortunate enough to be none the worse.

On November 20th, we gave the 5th Dragoon Guards back the horses we had borrowed from them, and received 52 remounts.

On the 21st, the 5th Dragoon Guards marched out of Pretoria for five days, going in the direction of Springs, but had an uneventful trek.

On the 25th, the following extracts from the "Gazette" were published:—

War Office, October 22nd.—Lieut. J. F. Church to be Captain, dated 1st July, 1901.

War Office, October 25th.—Lieut. A. Symons to be Captain, dated 5th October, 1901.

On the 29th, the following extracts from the "Gazette" of Sepember 27th, 1901, were published:—

13th Hussars.

To be Companions of the Distinguished Service Order:—
  Major (now Lieut.-Col.) Walter Charles Smithson.
  Captain (now Major) Kenneth McLaren.
  Captain Augus Howard Reginald Ogilvy.

To have the Distinguished Conduct Medal.
  Sergt. W. Mahon (since deceased).
  Private S. Herbert.
  Private E. Servey.

The squadron were doing as much musktry practise as possible, and had riding drills for remounts daily.

On November 30th, a very successful gymkhana was organized by the column, which was attended by all the rank and fashion of Pretoria.

On December 2nd, Lieut. Gubbins, who had injured his back at the gymkhana, had to go to hospital, and he was not fit to return for duty with the Regiment till June.

Brigadier-General Hamilton presented good conduct medals to Lce.-Corpl. Chesterman and Pte. G. Crook.

140   13th HUSSARS.

Lieut. R. St. C. Houstan went to hospital, and did not rejoin us.

We had taken over 102 horses from the 5th Dragoon Guards, and paraded to march out of Pretoria to Erstefabriken after dinner, on December 5th, with 12 Officers, and 587 W.O.s, and N.C.O.s, and Men.

The 5th Dragoon Guards turned out and gave us a great send off, on our leaving the column, wishing us as we wished them, every success. Lord Kitchener and General G. Hamilton rode out about four miles.

On December 6th, marched to Witfontein (536).

On December 7th, marched via Bronkhorst Spruit to Wilge River Bridge, passing the graves of the officers and men of the 94th Regiment, who were killed on December 20th, 1880.

On December 8th, a long march. It was intended to go to Grootspan (389), but we got too far to the north, near Brugspruit Station.

On December 9th, marched to Grootspan (389), and were joined by 150 surrendered burghers.

The Regiment, with these Boers, turned out at 8.45 p.m., for a night march, leaving the camp standing.

On December 10th (the next morning), the only four Boers that were seen were captured, and the Regiment returned to camp about 1 p.m., having got into communication with Urmston's Column.

On December 11th, Lieut. Elliott and half B Squadron with Captain Wood, and some men of the S.A.C., went out to Vlakvarkfontein (101), and came in contact with a superior force of Boers.

SOUTH AFRICAN WAR 141

The Regiment turned out to their assistance, and drove the Boers off, capturing one prisoner.

On December 12th, moved forward towards the Oliphant's River, and camped at Klip Pan (284).

On December 13th, Lieut.-Col. Smithson took out A and B Squadrons at 5 a.m. to cover the S.A.C., making new posts.

Captain Tremayne went into the line sick, and Lieut. J. T. Wigan took over command of C Squadron.

Orders were received to go west, after Boers who had broken through the S.A.C. posts on the 10th.

On December 14th, marched to Zaaiwater (184).

The following extracts from the "Gazette" were published for information:—

> The promotions to the rank of Lieutenants of the undermentioned 2nd Lieutenants, are ante dated as follows:—
>
> - T. E. Lambert, to June 9th, 1901, vice E. W. Denny, appointed Adjutant.
> - F. W. V. Cosens, to 1st July, 1901, vice J. F. Church, promoted.
> - Lieut. E. W. Denny to be Adjutant, vice J. H. Tremayne, who has vacated that appointment.

On December 15th, marched at 5 a.m. for Kromdrai (100). About mid-day C Squadron in advance, came in touch with some Boers, and were sent round by the right in order to try and cut them off, and A Squadron was sent round by the left.

C Squadron's advance was stopped by about 200 Boers, coming under a heavy fire, lost two horses, and Pte. Guest (whose horse was killed) was taken prisoner, but liberated immediately.

Sergt. Priddle stopped, under a heavy fire, and took up a man whose horse had been shot.

Pte. Young, whose horse pecked badly, came off, and got hung up in his stirrup. Lieut. J. T. Wigan went back under a heavy fire, and helped him to mount.

A Squadron galloped the hill where the Boers had laagered. The enemy had left a small rear guard, which cleared on the approach of the squadron, and on gaining this position the main body could be seen trekking away in the distance.

On December 16th, marched at 5 a.m. Lieut. Marchant captured six Boers in a farm-house, and a wounded Boer was found during the day.

A party of the Boers, in trying to avoid us, ran up against the 5th Dragoon Guards. Camped at Leeuwpoort (118).

On December 17th, marched to Springs. The guide, who, apparently, only had a rough idea of the country, took the Regiment about eight miles out of its way.

On December 18th, left Springs at 2.30 p.m., and marched to Modderfontein, where the 5th Dragoon Guards were encamped.

On December 19th, 13th and 5th Dragoon Guards marched to Witklip (702).

Information was received of Boers to the north.

On December 20th, marched at 1 a.m., picking up the 5th Dragoon Guards, to Blesbokfontein (533) and saw 30 or 40 Boers in the distance. Marched from Blesbokfontein to Weltervreden (532), near Kroomdrai (100) A very long day.

On December 21st, A Squadron went out to Vlakpan to reconnoitre, and later half C Squadron turned out, but saw no Boers.

On December 22nd, marched to Goedgevonden (23) near Zaaiwater.

On December 23rd, Major Williams took the Regiment to Vlakvarkfontein (101); B Squadron in advance. Some Boers were seen at Boochpoort (336) across the river, and Lieut. Pepys, with B Squadron, went for them.

The Boers cleared from the farm, but left a strong rear guard, who fired heavily on the squadron, but when it got over the river they galloped off, and were pursued for about five miles past the Silver Mines, where the Boers made a slight stand, but cleared when the supporting squadrons came up, leaving 93 head of cattle in our hands. Our horses were beat, and further pursuit was useless.

The Regiment started to return to Brugspruit about 3.30 p.m., and arrived to within a mile of the camp at 10 p.m., but, owing to the mist, they could not find the camp, and bivouacked for the night.

The Officer Commanding complimented B Squadron on the good work they had done during the day.

On December 24th, the Regiment moved into camp in the morning, and found Allenby's Column there.

We replaced the Greys, and Lieut.-Col. Smithson assumed command of the column. Colonel Allenby being away on sick leave.

Captains Tremayne and Church and Lieut. Kennard rejoined from hospital.

Captain Church took over command of A Squadron.

Lieut. J. T. Wigan was posted to C Squadron, and Lieut. C. E. Jenkins took over the duties of transport officer.

The following extract from the "Gazette," dated 26th November, 1901, is published for information 13th Hussars:—

Lieut. E. W. Denny, Adjutant, to be Captain, to complete establishment.

2nd Lieut. C. E. Jenkins to be Lieutenant, vice A. Symons, promoted.

December 25th, Christmas Day. The "Peace on Earth" part of the Christmas programme seemed to be obsolete.

Presents were received from Lady Russell and other friends at home, from the Reserve Squadron, and from the "Morning Post," for which we were very grateful, and sincerely hoped that we should not have to tax their generosiy another year.

The officers of the Greys and Carabiniers came round to see us, and we had a cheery evening.

On December 26th, the Greys left in the morning, and the Carabiniers marched to the junction of the Oliphant's River and Steenkool Spruit.

The staff of the column was:—

Colonel Allenby, Commanding.
Lieut. Gibb, Inniskillings, A.D.C.
Captain P. J. Bayley, 12th Lancers, Brigade Major.
Major E. A. Maude, Scots Greys, A.P.M.
Lieut. White, R.E., Intelligence Officer.

The column consisted of:—

The Carabiniers, Major Butler, Commanding.
13th Hussars, Lieut.-Col. Smithson, D.S.O.
Four companies Durham Light Infantry, Major Saunders.
Pom-pom, Captain Smith.

December 27th, marched at 8 a.m., and joined the Carabiniers at the junction of the Oliphant's River and Steenkool Spruit.

On December 28th, the Brigade marched to Onverwacht (478). The Steenkool Spruit was very full, and in crossing the drift at the end of the march the hospital tonga was carried away, and the ponies drowned.

C Squadron was left at Steenkoll Spruit for convoy duty.

On December 30th, the Regiment marched at 1 a.m., and bivouacked near Bethel, capturing two prisoners on the way, the only two Boers seen, though Bethel reported that they were very numerous in the vicinity.

On December 31st, the Regiment returned to Onverwacht (478) where C Squadron, less Lieut. Kennard, and his troop (who was left at Steenkool Spruit), rejoined.

During the year the deaths in the Regiment were as follows:—

Killed and died of wounds	12
Enteric	15
Dysentry	1
Other Causes	1
	29

143 men were invalided home, and 419 N.C.O.'s and men joined with different drafts.

On January 2nd, the camp remained standing. C Squadron went out to look for a gun captured from Benson's column, and said to be in a spruit, but did not find it.

The strength of the Regiment at the front on January 1st, 1902, was:—

13 Officers, 394 N.C.O.'s and Men, and 393 horses.

At the details there were:—

Two Officers, and 231 N.C.O.'s and Men.

SOUTH AFRICAN WAR.

And the total strength in South Africa was:—

832 N.C.O.'s and Men, 119 of whom were in various hospitals.

January 2nd, marched to Vaalkop. A few Boers were seen on the hills, but they retired before the advanced guard.

On January 3rd—4th, remained at Vaalkop, and sent the wagons into Steenkool Spruit for supplies.

On January 5th, the Regiment, under Major Williams, turned out at midnight 4th—5th, and marched on Bultfontein (217) arriving there at dawn. The three squadrons advanced on the farm from different directions, but found no Boers, and, just as we thought that we had toiled all night, and caught nothing, a patrol on the left sent in to say that they could see a lot of cattle in a farm over a ridge beyond us. The Regiment went on, and seeing about 80 to 100 Boers leaving the farm, immediately pursued, and captured 11 prisoners, including Commandant Breytenbach, and ex-Commandant Woolman; also 600 head of cattle, 30 ponies, 60 mules, and six Cape carts. On the way back to camp, about 30 Boers attacked our rear and left, and a smart rear guard action took place for a considerable distance, during which No. 3563 Sergt. Hetherington, and No. 3350 Pte .Cleaver were wounded.

C Squadron had the luck to see the Boers first in the morning, and perhaps, had somewhat the best of the gallop, but A and B Squadrons had the fighting when we retired.

Captain Tremayne was especially recommended by

Lieut.-Colonel Smithson for the good work he had done, and for the single handed capture of Commandant Breytenbach (who was one of the Boers hardest fighting generals). Captain Tremayne, who was better mounted than the men of his squadron, pursued and captured him (vide February 12th).

January 6th, remained at Vaalkop. One section 66th Battery, R.F.A., joined the column.

On January 7th, marched at 7 a.m. to Yzerwarkvontein (121). On arrival in camp, a party was sent out to search for a gun captured from Benson's column on October 30th, and it was found in a spruit about two miles off, and brought back to camp riddled with bullets, but none the worse for its two months' immersion.

On January 8th, marched at 4.30 a.m. to Onverwacht (478), capturing five Boers on the way.

January 9th, remained at Onverwacht. A draft of 50 N.C.O.'s and men arrived, and were posted to the different squadrons.

The Carabineers made a night march, and came upon some Boers in the morning, whom they pursued for a

long way to the Wilge River, but could not come up to them.

On January 10th, marched to Steenkool Spruit.

On January 11th, remained at Steenkool Spruit. Colonel Allenby rejoined, and resumed command of the Regiment, and Lieut.-Col. Smithson resumed command of the Regiment.

On January 12th, returned to Vaal Kop, and remained halted there on the 13th.

On January 14th, started at 8 a.m. for Steenkool Spruit, but received orders by helio on the way to go to Bethel. Camped at Yzerwarkfontein (121).

On January 15th, Colonel Allenby rode into Bethel for orders from General Bruce Hamilton.

About 11 a.m. camp was moved to Drifontein, south of Vaal Kop, where we could see about 40 Boers, whom we shelled off the hill.

On January 16th, returned to Steenkool Spruit, B and C Squadrons, under Major Williams, started about 11 p.m. for a night march. However, early the next morning a Kaffir told us that the Boers were also night marching, and had trekked shortly after sunset on January 16th, so we returned to camp.

On January 18th, we remained at Steenkool Spruit till the 22nd.

On the 19th, B Squadron went into Brugspruit with the convoy, and returned the following day. On the 20th, C Squadron turned out early, and went out in the direction of Captain Oliver's S.A.C. post, to support the Carabiniers, who had gone out the night before, if required, but returned in the middle of the day without having seen a Boer.

On the 18th, A Squadron were out all the afternoon destroying mealies, etc.

On January 20th, the details trained from Pretoria to Standerton, and remained there until the conclusion of hostilities. While at Standerton, the whole of Gen. Bruce Hamilton's details were under the command of Lieut.-Colonel Jenner, D.S.O.,

On January 22nd, marched back to Vaal Kop.

On January 23rd, remained at Vaal Kop all day, and started at 8 p.m. for a night march.

On January 24th, at dawn, we crossed the Olifant River, and marched past Vlaklaagte (180) and came in touch with the other columns working under General Bruce Hamilton, and returned to camp at Vlaklaagte (180).

Early in the morning it was reported that an officer of the Durham Light Infantry was missing, so about 8 a.m. a patrol, under Sergt. White, was sent back to Vaal Kop to look for him. Sergt. White left two men at the drift just short of the Kop, and going on with the other two men, saw a party of about a dozen Boers on the hill. Leaving the horses at the foot of the hill he crept up with one man, and opened fire on the Boers, who fled. He then retired on the drift, and the Boers, discovering the smallness of his party, tried to gallop round, and cut him off, but, on coming under fire from the two men left at the drift they fell back, and Sergt. White returned to the Regiment without having seen anything of the missing officer.

On the 25th, remained in camp till 3 p.m., when 200 men of the 13th Hussars and 200 men of the Carabiniers turned out, the remainder being left with Major Williams to bring the baggage along.

The column marched past Wing's camp, and halted

there for about an hour, nd then went on, and about midnight surrounded three farms, with no success.

On January 26th, about 3 a.m., we came up with General Bruce Hamilton, who had Spens' Column of Mounted Infantry with him, and McKenzie's Column. We then changed our direction, and at about 4.30 a.m. —in a fine open bit of country—we came upon the Bethel and Ermelo Commandos at Springbokfontein (36), and after a good gallop took many prisoners, and all their cattle and wagons.

We then marched to Ermelo and bivouacked, the horses having been under the saddle for 23 hours. It was raining when we turned out, and rained continually till we got to Ermelo.

The total number of prisoner captured by General Bruce Hamilton during this night was just under one hundred.

On January 27th, the baggage arrived about 2 p.m., Boers had hung around it nearly the whole way, and several skirmishes had taken place. We pitched our camp near the fort.

On January 28th remained at Ermelo. The horses badly wanted a day's rest.

On January 29th, the camp was shifted about three miles to Jan Hendrickfontein (18).

Major Williams, who was unwell, stayed at Ermelo, and went into Standerton with the first convoy. He was appointed C.S.O., to General Elliot, dated 24th February, 1902, and rejoined the Regiment at Pretoria after the declaration of peace.

General Bruce Hamilton published the following telegram and order:—

"Telegram from Lord Kitchener.

"I am more than pleased at your continued success. Congratulate all ranks from me on their perseverance and dash under such trying circumstances."

The G.O.C. has great pleasure in communicating the above to the troops, and wishes to express his own approbation of the cheerful spirit they show under constant and trying work, which entails considerable hardships, but which they have the satisfaction of knowing is of great service to the nation, and goes far towards ending the war.

The columns now at Ermelo were Allenby's, McKenzie's Spens', and the J.M.R.s. All the columns were formed into three lines, as follows:—

A line .... The Fighting Force.
B line Wagons on a light scale and escort.
C line .... Heavy baggage, etc.

January 30th, at 6.45 p.m., Allenby's and Mackenzie's Columns, and the J.M.R.s, under General Bruce Hamilton, started out for a night march. After our recent success we were all extra keen, especially as Col. Wools Samson, who had been so invaluable as an intelligence officer, was with us, and Louis Botha was supposed to be in the vicinity.

About 11 p.m., we crossed the Vaal by a pontoon bridge, and marched at a tremendous pace till daylight.

Two or three farms were searched, but with no success, nor were any of the enemy seen at all.

It had been a very wet night, and everybody was soaked to the skin.

We bivouacked at Schimmelhoek (89), and the B Line, which started at 3 a.m., arrived about 2 p.m.

On February 1st marched at 9 a.m., for about seven or eight miles, and bivouacked at Waaihoek (170). No tents were allowed to be put up, and we were off again at 4.45 p.m., and marched through the night to Athole (85), but were unsuccessful in finding Boers.

On February 2nd, we bivouacked at Athole (85), and B Line arrived about 4 p.m.

On February 3rd, marched to Newcastle (237) starting about 9 a.m.

On February 4th, marched to Ban Kop, and A Line started off again at 6.30 p.m., and marched all through the night with hardly a halt.

At dawn we were somewhere in the vicinity of Ringknik (207), and the scouts reported two Boers a short distance ahead of us. The whole force pushed on, and a Boer convoy was seen about five miles off, but our horses were too beat to go on. A Squadron caught two Boers hiding in the rocks, and McKenzie's Column, on our right, got five prisoners, and four wagons, and about 800 head of cattle was driven in. The J.M.R.s killed a Boer. About 6.30 a.m., the columns marched back to Westoe (250), where they found Line B.

This was a very hard day and night. The horses had been under the saddle about 20 hours, and had covered not far short of 60 miles.

On February 6th, rest day. The horses badly wanted a rest.

On February 7th, the force marched past Newcastle, (237) to Ban Kop.

Barter's Column arrived, bringing us supplies.

The force remained at Ban Kop till the 16th, being supplied from Ermelo.

February 12th, the following extracts were published in the "London Gazette":—

"13th Hussars.

"Captain E. W. N. Pedder to be Major, vice McLaren, D.S.O., placed on temporary half-pay, dated November 1st, 1901."

"Army Orders of 1st February, 1902.

"Captain J. H. Tremayne to be Brevet-Major, for the single handed capture of Commandant Breytenbach, and general good service.

We turned out for a night march at 7 p.m., but the night was so wet and misty that Col. Wools Sampson's boys declined to be responsible for the correct guiding of the force, so we turned in again.

Februry 15th, Major Maude, A.P.M., left the column to rejoin his regiment, Captain Vandeleur replacing him.

February 16th, McKenzie's and Allenby's Columns marched at 4 a.m.

Colonel Spens' Column was in the vicinity, and the the three columns were under his direction. We camped near Lake Banagher.

Just before getting into camp a lot of cattle were reported about three miles off, but on going out to drive them in, it was found that it was a large herd of blesbok.

On February 17th, the orders were for the camp to stand, and a force of about 50 men per squadron were to be ready to march at 4 a.m.

A force of Boers was reported to be at Lettieskeus (36), and it was Colonel Spens' intention to drive this party on to the Ermelo-Bankop block-houses. However, it was a foggy morning, and therefore these operations were abandoned.

February 28th, the column marched at 6.45 p.m., and about 3 a.m. (18th) surrounded a farm, Hol Nek (41), on foot, but found no Boers. We marched on again, and at dawn found ourselves overlooking the Koomati Valley, a very rough and hilly country.

McKenzie's Column made a detour, and caught 12 prisoners.

We went back to Vlackfontein (46), where the baggage joined us in the afternoon.

February 19th, a short march to Uitkyk (189), where we stayed till the 24th. On the 20th, Colonel Spens' Column came in.

On the 21st, the wagons were sent into Carolina for supplies. At midnight 22nd—23rd 125 men from each regiment marched out in different directions. At dawn we saw two or three Boers in the distance.

McKenzie's Column had been luckier, and had caught nine Boers, including Grobelaar's brother. Grobelaar himself escaped. We got back to camp about 11 a.m.

February 24th, marched to Lake Banagher. We got into camp, and were grooming our horses, when a herd of blesbok galloped between us and McKenzie's Column, who immediately began firing at them. They only killed two deer, though doubtless many were wounded. However, they succeeded in stampeding several horses of other units, and wounded a few. Fortunately, we never came across any more blesbok while working with McKenzie's Column.

February 25th, marched to Roodeval (93). Here we got some remounts. Vet.-Lieutenant Durrant, A.V.D., joined us.

February 24th, a long march in a thick fog to De Emigratie (27).

February 27th, marched to Rolfontein (261).

Plumer's and Campbell's Columns were close to us.

February 28th, marched to Wydgeleden (306). Botha was supposed to be in the vicinity of Vryheid, and about 10 columns were to operate against him.

On March 1st, marched to Wakkerstroom, where we heard that the drive that had just taken place in the O.R.C. had resulted in the loss to the Boers of over

600 men, and a vast quantity of cattle, etc. Marched to Groenvlei (46).

On March 3rd. a thick fog. Marched to Boschoek (183). McKenzie's Column followed us up a day or two behind.

On March 4th, the ox convoy started at 4 a.m., with an escort, under Lieut.-Col. Smithson, consisting of A and B Squadrons, 13th Hussars, and 200 of the Carabiniers. The remainder of the column marched at 6.30 a.m., and got into camp at Zoetmelksrivier (86) about 12 noon.

Shortly after arriving in camp, some of the J.M.R.'s, who had gone out raiding, were severely sniped, but the guns and pom-poms from camp soon drove off the few Boers that were about.

On March 5th, Spens' Column marched to Vryheid. We marched through Pivaan's Poort to Marthinus Drift over the Pivaan River.

On March 6th, marched at 5.30 a.m. to Welverdiend (194) and pitched camp.

About 4.30 p.m., the Regiment moved off, and took up a position on the south side of the river, near Pivaan's Bridge.

On the 7th March, we shifted our positon at daylight the next morning, and about 1 p.m. the rest of the column came up, and camped on the high ground south of Pivaan's Bridge.

On the 8th March, B Squadron and some of C Squadron escorted a convoy as far as Vaalbank (205) on its way to Vryheid, and returned to camp about 2 p.m.

On March 9th, marched at 9 a.m. to Voorkemplaats (332). A very cramped camp in very long grass, and many kraals about, in every one of which there was said to be small-pox.

Marched about 1 p.m. on 10th, when we got to Alman's Nek. The Carabiniers branched off, and escorted a convoy to Vryheid. We marched on, and camped at Welgevonden (287) after dark.

On 11th, marched at 5 a.m., to Vaalbank (430) arriving about 9 a.m. The Carabiniers returned with the convoy.

Lieut. Elliot went sick wth measles, and returned to duty on April 15th, at Standerton.

On the 12th, the column marched at 7 a.m., C Squadron escorting the convoy, marching at 5 a.m. We got into camp at Metselfontein (499) shortly after, having gone over a very rough and hilly road.

Spens' Column, with General Bruce Hamilton, camped about three miles to the north of us.

On the 13th, Line A marched at 2 a.m. to Spens' camp, and then waited till dawn. We then went on about three miles, and were ordered to take a high hill. Spens' Mounted Infantry on the left, ourselves in the centre, and the J.M.R.'s on the right. A and B Squadrons had a stiff climb, and found nothing when they got to the top.

We returned about noon to Reddersdal (339), and camped.

On the 14th, marched at 7 a.m. to Geluk (234), and were off again at 7 p.m. We went over a very rough bit of country, and being in rear of the column had an awful luggage train march all through the night. About midnight the column ran into General Cherry Emmett, and a Boer corporal, and captured them. Shortly after this Lieut. Hodgkinson and his troop were sent off with the A.P.M., Captain Vandeleur, and they ran up against a good many Boers, who opened a hot fire. It was pitch dark, so Lieut. Hodgkinson had to retire. No. 3554 Lance-Corporal Dennis was wounded in the thigh. From the effects of this wound, which did not seem serious at the time, he was invalided home, and subsequently discharged as medically unfit for further service. The Carabiniers, who had also made a detour, also found some Boers, and had two men wounded.

On the 15th, the native scouts reported a few Boers on our left. C Squadron went on, and captured two or three prisoners, and drove a few more into the J.M.R.s.

When all the parties collected later on at Prodger's Farm (Broeders Rust 144), where we bivouacked, it was found that five Boers had been killed, four wounded, and 19 unwounded prisoners had been captured, and a lot of cattle was driven in.

On the 16th, we marched to Reddersdal (329), and found Line B there. A long and hilly march, and the pace had to be slow, as the wounded had to be carried on extemporised stretchers, the country being much too rough for ambulances.

On the 17th, we were in readiness to start out again at 6.15 p.m., but the order was cancelled.

On 18th, A Line marched at 7 p.m.

Lieut. Wigan, with Lieut. Hodgkinson and 60 specially selected men and horses from the Regiment, and some J.M.R.s and Carabiniers, went off by themselves with Lieut. J. Mossop (Intelligence Department) and Guide Nicol. This party, after pushing on as rapidly as possible over a very rough and hilly country all through the night, got information from natives at dawn that Louis Botha was not far off. On arriving Potgeiter's Farm (Hlomo-Hlomo) they were told that he had left about 20 minutes before they arrived, and they again pushed on, but the horses were getting very tired, so they soon had to abandon further pursuit, and rejoined the column during the afternoon. The column marched through the night, and just before dawn climbed up an awful mountain and down the other side, when we found ourselves in a hilly bush country, with a quantity of cattle about. The J.M.R.s and Mounted Infantry pushed on, and thoroughly searched the kloofs in the vicinity, but very few Boers were seen, though we got a lot of their cattle, which were in beautiful condition.

On the 19th, about 11 a.m., our column went on to Hlomo-Hlomo, and bivouacked, being joined there by the J.M.R.'s and M.I.

A Squadron, who had been sent out to search some caves, did not get in till after 6 p.m., after a very hard day's climbing up steep mountain sides covered with bush.

During the day six Boers were captured.

On the 20th, the force marched at 7.30 a.m. to Toovernars Rust (58). About 18 miles, and very steep ones, too.

About 10.30 a.m. the force off saddled for about two hours, and it was understood that Dinnizulu was coming out to meet General Bruce Hamilton. However, the day was too wet for him, and he did not turn up.

On the 21st, there was a General parade of the column, for General Bruce Hamilton to present the D.S.O. to Lieut.-Col. Smithson.

So confident were we that there would not be a night march, that we spent the afternoon playing stump cricket.

However, about 7 p.m. an order came for Line A to turn out at once. Lieut. Wigan, with 60 specially selected men and horses from the Regiment, and a like number from the Carabiniers, went on ahead of the force, and marched to Hlomo-Hlomo, but found no one in the farm, so went on to the hills beyond, and unearthed five Boers out of a cave, one of them being Potgeiter, the owner of the farm, and another an Irishman named O'Conner, who had donned a red cross badge for the occasion. We off saddled for about four hours, and then returned to the camp we had left.

On the 23rd, Spens' and McKenzie's Columns

marched about 7 a.m., and we marched about 9 a.m., and camped near Metselfontein (499).

The following order was published for information, and it was gratifying to know that the difficult nature of the country that we had been working in was recognized.

> "The Maj.-General Commanding has great pleasure in communicating to the troops under his command the following telegram from the Commander-in-Chief:—
>
> "Tell your troops how highly I appreciate their work in so difficult a country."

Lieut. H. J. J. Stern took over command of B Squadron, and Lieut. Pepys took up the duties of Adjutant on the 25th, during the temporary absence of Captain Denny, who proceeded down country on leave. We were now joined by a Zulu Impi (Tabakulu's Impi), about 800 strong, who marched along with us.

We received a wire from our old friends, the 5th Dragoon Guards, in reply to a message we had sent them, wishing them "Good Luck" on leaving the country for India.

On the 24th, remained halted.

On 25th, marched to Vaalbank (430).

On the 26th, marched to Vryheid.

From here 40 men were sent down country to proceed to India, to join the 4th Hussars.

Civil-Surgeon Whyte went sick with measles, and did

SOUTH AFRICAN WAR.   163

not rejoin the Regiment. 2nd Lieut. R. B. B. Baggallay joined.

On the 27th, the column marched to Alman's Nek (114). Lieut. Hodgkinson and 50 men were left behind to escort General Bruce Hamilton.

Vcty.-Lieut. Durrant left to proceed to India. 2nd Lieut. W. F. Black, attached to the Leicester Regiment, was gazetted to us, but was invalided home before joining, and did not join the Regiment till April, 1903.

On the 28th, marched to Bedrog (571) where General Bruce Hamilton passed through, and went on to Paulpietersberg.

On the 29th, marched to Paulpietersberg, where Spens' and McKenzie's Columns were camped. Colville's Column left in the morning. At 4 p.m., the column marched again a short distance to Halberton (19).

The Carabiniers went out for a night march.

On the 30th, marched at 3 a.m., and crossed the Pivaan River about 7.30 a.m., at Martinus Drift. Here we outspanned till 10 a.m., when we went on through the Poort, and camped at Mooihoek (54), where the Carabiniers, who had had no luck, joined us.

There was a little sniping going through the Poort. An old man and his two sons were supposed to live amongst the rocks and amuse themselves by sniping the columns as they came through. Cherry Emmett had told us that the Boers would like to get hold of these three men as much as we should, as they had absolutely refused to go on commando, and never could be found when sent for.

On the 31st, marched to Boschhoek (183).

On April 1st, marched to Groenvlei (46).

On the 2nd, marched to Wakkerstroom. Civil surgeon Stewart joined.

On the 3rd, remained halted. Trekking did not, apparently, agree with the cricket of Allenby's Column. We played the North Staffordshire, and got a bad beating.

Lieut. Jenkins went to hospital with jaundice.

On the 4th, the column left Wakkerstroom, and marched to Ermelo, camping on the 4th at Driefontein (231), on the 5th at Berginderlin Bridge on the Vaal, and arrived at Ermelo on the 6th.

On the 7th, remained at Ermelo, and got 70 horses and 71 men from the details.

On the 8th, marched to Carolina, camping on the 8th at Welgelagen (186), on the 9th at Bothwell, and arriving on the 10th at Carolina.

Each squadron detailed a party to collect as much wire as possible, to be used for defensive purposes at night, during the forthcoming drive.

On the 11th, the columns taking part in this drive were Park's, Williams', Wing's, Spens', McKenzie's, Allenby's; Stewart with the J.M.R.s.

On the 11th, we got into positon as follows:—
- The left of Park's Column at Goodhoop (378).
- The left of Williams' Column at Klipfontein (210).
- The left of Wing's Column at Speculatie (246).
- The left of Spens' Column at Shoonoord (430).
- The left of McKenzie's Column at Helpmaakar (20).
- The left of Allenby's Column at Bosmanspruit, west of Carolina.
- And the J.M.R.s continuing on to the Carolina-Ermelo blockhouse line.

Thus the line of the drive began from Great Ollifant's Station to Carolina, and it was to work down to the railway line.

The pace was to be taken from Spens' Column, and the order of march was B and C Squadrons in extended formation in front, and one squadron (A) in support.

No fires were allowed till it was light, and this made cooking difficult, as we did not get anything to cook till it was dark during the drives.

C Squadron, on the right, was responsible for keeping touch with the Carabiniers.

At night the supporting squadrons came up into line, and a long continuous chain of outposts was formed.

On the 12th, at 6.30 a.m., the line advanced, and marched on during the day with one short halt, till 4 p.m., only seeing a few scattered Boers. An order had been given out that the whole line would halt at 10.30 a.m., but as Spens' Column did not halt,

we all had to march on till nearly noon before we got
our halt. At night the left of the columns were as
follows:—

    Park, at Welstand (129).
    Williams, at Kleinfontein (269).
    Wing, at Weltervonden (179).
    Spens, at Shoonoord (430).
    McKenzie, at Boschmanskop (263).
    Allenby, at Vogelfontein (4).
    Stewart continuing to the blockhouse line.

The distance that Allenby's Column marched (for
those that went the nearest way), was rather over 20
miles.

On arriving at our position, each squadron had a
certain length of the line assigned to it, and set to
work to entrench the posts, and put up wire entangle-
ments, etc., in front of them.

There was a good deal of firing all along the line
during the night, the Boers evidently feeling along the
line for a gap.

On the 13th, started at 6.30 a.m., in the same order,
and marched about 25 miles, getting into our position
between 4 and 5 p.m. We marched over burnt veldt
nearly the whole day, with a strong wind in our faces.
We saw very few Boers again this day. During the
night a lot of ponies were galloping backwards and
forwards in front of the line. Whether the Boers had
driven them down on us to see what the effect would
be, is not known, but it encouraged musketry, which
continued most of the night. The next morning two

or three dead ponies were found in front of our line, and during the day more wounded ones were found and destroyed.

We afterwards heard that a considerable number of Boers had broken back through Spens and McKenzie.

The positions of the column for the night was:—
Park, at Frischgevaad (178).
Williams, at Elandsfontein (102).
Wing, at G.G., three miles south of Bethel.
Spens, at Bekkersrust.
McKenzie, at Oshoek (33).
Allenby, at Uitzuicht (32).
Stewart continuing on to the blockhouse line.

On the 14th, started at 6 a.m., marched to Standerton, a march of about 40 miles.

Again, only a few Boers were seen. We got in about 6 p.m. very tired, and the horses all dead beat, and found that Captain Battye and Lieut. and Qrmr. Rupert had done much to promote our comfort on arrival in camp, a little distance outside the town.

On the 15th, the baggage arrived during the morning, and the following telegram from General Bruce Hamilton was published:—

"Result of drive.
Killed 1
Wounded Prisoners 1
Unwounded Prisoners 134
Cape Carts 2
Rifles 85
S.A.A. 4800
and a good many horses.

Colonel Long, R.A., employed on the Remount Department, inspected the horses and though the number of horses we had been obliged to destroy during the drive was very small, the number to go to the Sick Horse Depot and details for rest, amounted to 140, and after getting all available horses from the details, the strength of the Regiment on leaving Standerton on the 17th was only 320 N.C.O.s and men.

A six months' issue of clothing was issued out to the men here.

The following extract from the "Gazette" was published for information:—

"War Office, March 18th.

"13th Hussars.

Lieut. H. J. J. Stern to be Captain, vice A. Symons seconded.

The promotion to the rank of Lieutenant of 2nd Lieut. G. Halswelle is ante-dated to January 22nd, 1902, vice H. J. J. Stern.

2nd Lieut. W. A. Kennard to be Lieutenant, vice F. G. Bayley, seconded.

2nd Lieut. Elliot rejoined from hospital, and Capt. Denny from leave.

On the 16th, marched at 2 p.m. through the town to Boschoff's Farm on the Brakspruit. Lt.-Col. Smithson, D.S.O., who had been unwell for some days, went down country on sick leave, which left Major Tremayne in command of the Regiment. Lieut. Wigan took over command of C Squadron.

Captain Stern went down country on leave, and Lieut Pepys took over command of B Squadron.

On the 17th, marched at 7.30 a.m. across the Vaal, and got into camp about 4 p.m. at Grasptaatz, south of the Vaal. A few Boers followed the rear guard up (Lieut. Hodgkinson), and he was slightly annoyed for a few miles, but when the pom-pom was sent back to him the Boers drew off

On the 18th, marched at 6.30 a.m. to Van Wyks' Vlei. A good many Boers were about, and there was sniping on all sides of the column at different times during the day.

On the 19th, marched to Villiersdorp, and camped on the high ground on the south side of the river, overlooking the dorp.

The afternoon was spent in building entrenched posts round the camp, and this was continued for the next two or three days.

About 9.30 p.m., a sharp fire opened from the Boers all round the camp. The men turned out very quickly and lined the outskirts of the camp, and kept up a rapid fire for a few minutes, the guns and pom-poms joining in. This stopped the Boers fire, which broke out again in a desultory manner once or twice, but after an hour they gave it up altogether. The Carnbiniers had two men wounded by one of the Kaffir scouts, and we had two horses hit. The J.M.R.s had a few casualties among their horses.

On the 20th, 200 men of the Regiment, and 100 Carabiniers escorted the convoy into Frankfort, returning the next day.

While the convoy was out-spanned on the return journey, several mules showed symptoms of severe illness, two dying in a very short time. The Conductors said that it was caused by the "bossie worm," another of the very many evils that animals have to contend against in that country.

On the 23rd, 200 from the Carabiniers, and 200 of us, with the pom-pom, made a reconnaissance on the north side of the river to the Hex Rivier.

There were a few Boers there, and one Carabinier was wounded. The Regiment did not get in till about 6 p.m., as it had to escort the pom-pom and ambulance back by a drift some way round. About 40 Boers were seen on the way home, but they kept at a respectful distance.

On the 25th, at 6 a.m., the convoy marched into Frankfort with 200 Carabiniers and 100 13th Hussars.

About noon, orders were received to march at 2 p.m. with all available horsts, no transport, and to leave the camp standing. Lieut. Pepys was left with a party to guard the camp. Major Prendergast, second in command of the J.M.R.s, being in command of the details.

About 2.45 p.m., about 30 Carabiniers, about 150 13th Hussars, and about 150 J.M.R.s marched out along the Heidelberg road.

At 6.30 p.m., we halted till 9 p.m., and then

moved on again till 4.15 a.m. (26th), and halted just over the Zuicherbosch River to the east of Da Hoek. At daylight the J.M.R.s found seven Boers in a farm close by, and we went on to Heidelberg, where we bivouacked.

This was a long march of about 45 miles.

On the 27th, marched at 7 a.m. for Vlakfontein, which we reached about 2 p.m.

In the evening, the 7th, Bays, and Greys marched in after an unsuccessful drive.

On the 28th, marched at 6.30 a.m., and reached Villiersdorp about 3 p.m., about 25 miles. During the day we came across a Boer despatch rider, who said he had been riding about for two days looking for Boers to summon them to a peace (or war) meeting, and had been able to find none. He had a pass on him to allow him through our lines, so we gave him some food, and turned him loose.

From the 29th to May 2nd, rest days. The column had race meetings on the 29th and May 2nd.

On the 3rd, the Regiment moved out in the morning to get touch with Col. Duff's Column (Wing's Column— Wing was laid up with a broken collar bone), coming from Greylingstad. We went as far as Brandkraal (55) opposite Hex Rivier, and after a long wait saw the 8th coming along.

Lawley, Garrett, Spens, McKenzie, and Duff were driving down the railway line to the Frankfort and Heilbron line of block-houses. On getting touch with Duff's Column, we retired on Villiersdorp so as to prevent the enemy breaking away across their front, to the left, and the J.M.R.s moved towards Frankfort, followed by the Carabiniers, so that during the night the column might hold a line from Bendigo (61) to Frankfort. Owing to some misunderstanding the J.M.R.s went on into Frankfort, which left the Carabiniers an impossible line to hold, and during the night Ross' Commando, with their cattle, broke through.

The 8th Hussars, on the right, only about three troops, had also lost touch, so there was also a gap on our right.

On the 4th, the morning was very foggy, which delayed the start till about 7 a.m., and the column on our right was difficult to find. However, the drive was continued to the Frankfort Heilbron Blockhouse line, and we concentrated at Leuwspruit (576) about two miles to the west of Frankfort. The drive so far had resulted in the capture of 87 prisoners.

On the 5th, Lieut. Pepys, who had four months' leave to proceed to England, left for Heilbron.

On the 5th, most columns moved a short distance in the afternoon, so as to get into position to continue the drive south the following day.

The orders for the positions of the columns on the night of the 5th, were as follows:—

    Col. Rimington, right at Koppies Station.

    Col. Rimington, left on Rhenoster, due south of Dui Major Drift (626).

    Col. Lawley, on Elands Spruit, due north of Schurvekop (195).

Col. Nixon, at Midden Rust (478).
Col. Garrett, left near Somerset (107).
Col. Spens, at Welguluk (174).
Col.. McKenzie, at Holfontein (315).
Col. Duff, at Frischgevacht (623).
Col. Allenby, at Koppiesdam (690).

"On the following day the force will drive right out in one day to Lindley-Kroonsradt Blockhouse line. As soon as possible after starting the flanks of the column will gain touch with each other, and will maintain it throughout the day.

"Colonel Barker's and General Elliot's troops will hold the line of the Liebenberg Vlei from Frankfort to Halfman (84) and thence to Lindley, and the Lindley-Kroonstadt blockhouse line will be strengthened. Troops will drive right out to this line, with their flanks in touch till they reach there.. The positon of Colonel Allenby's Column on reaching this line will be with his left near Kromspruit (331), and in touch with General Elliot's troops. Colonel Garrett's left will direct throughout. The force will move at 5.30 a.m., and will halt for one hour at 10.30 a.m., at which hour Colonel Garrett must be at Mildrai (335)."

In accordance with the above orders, the column marched at 5.30 a.m. The 13th on the right, then the Carabiniers, and then the J.M.R.s on the left. When we got to within about three miles of General Elliot's line, we saw a large party of Boers, probably about 200, and thought that their capture was a certainty. About 25 of them turned away to our left, and tried to break through between the Carabiniers and the J.M.R.s, with the result that they had three killed and 17 taken prisoners. The remainder waited till we were getting pretty close, when, to everybody's astonishment, they galloped through the blocking line without a shot being fired at them—a disappointing finale to a 35 mile drive, which might have considerably increased the number of captures had not somebody blundered.

We bivouacked alongside General Elliot's troops.

On the 7th, all the troops moved towards Lindley at 7.30 a.m. Colonel Allenby's Column marched about six miles, and took over four days' supplies, and then marched back.

On the 8th, marched a short distance at 12.15 p.m., to get into position to drive back to Frankfort-Heilbron line of blockhouses.

On the 9th, the whole line was to advance at 5.30 a.m. At 4.45 a.m., Lieut. Elliot was sent out with his troop to get in touch with Colonel Duff's Column on our left, but it was not till 6.30 a.m. that they came up abreast of us, and we could move. About 10 a.m. Duff's Column halted, and reported that the troops on their left were a long way behind. About two hours were wasted in waiting, and then we dragged slowly on. There was a muddle somewhere, and the consequence was that at dusk we were still about 12 miles from Frankfort, and as it was no good driving in the dark, the column concentrated, and arrived at Frankfort about 9 p.m.

The result of these drives was 231 prisoners, and 11 killed.

On the 10th and 11th, the column remained at Frankfort.

The following telegram, dated May 7th, was received by Major-General Hamilton, from the G.O.C. Commander-in-Chief:—

"Tell your troops I am very pleased at good result of their hard work, and rely on all to do their best now, after which I hope to give them a good long rest."

On the 12th, the column marched about noon, en route for Greylingstad, camping at Bendigo (61), and burning all the veldt behind us.

The following order was issued:—

"Unless different orders are issued, the troops will not fire at the enemy unless the enmy takes the offensive."

The following extracts from the "Gazette" were published for information:—

"13th Hussars.—Lieuts. to be Captains, F. G. Bayley, in succession to Major E. A. Wigan, who holds an extra-regimental appointment: A. W. B. Spencer, vice Bayley, seconded for service on the staff 2nd Lieut. C. Elliot to be Lieutenant. vice Spencer (March 26th); William Henry Eve, University candidate. to be 2nd Lieutenant.—Dated 14th March, 1902."

The following extracts from Army Order 83 of 1902, was published:—

"List of N.C.O.s and men awarded medals for 'Long Service and Good Conduct.'

"13th Hussars.—No. 2570 S.Q.M.S. Page."

On 13th marched to Zand Drift.

The following extracts from Army Orders, dated March, 1902, were published for information:—

"The following have been brought to the notice of the G.O.C. Commanding in Chief:—

"No. 2586 S.S.M. F. G. Brown, 13th Hussars (13th Squadron, 5th Regiment, I.Y.), for good service and gallantry in action in an attack on a convoy near Klerksdorp, 25th February, 1902."

This N.C.O.s name appeared among the mentions in Lord Kitchener's despatch; dated June, 1902.

On the 14th, marched to Silverbank (140). The order to burn the veldt nearly cost us dearly this day. It was a windy day, and the fires spread rapidly. A wagon containing ammunition broke down, and this delayed the rear guard (Lieut. Elliot). The Boers crept up, under cover of the smoke, and captured one man on the flank, and then attacked the rear guard. However, Lieut. Elliot kept them off, and got the wagon in without assistance.

When the camp had been pitched, and the horses all in the lines, it was noticed that a fire was coming down straight for the camp. All the men were turned out to try and stop it at a small spruit below the camp, and the horses were got out of the lines. The fire, which came on at a very rapid rate, jumped the spruit, and luckily for us, only went through the corner of our camp, but it went right through the Carabiniers, burning tents, blankets, clothing, etc., and exploding the

SOUTH AFRICAN WAR. 177

ammunition in the bandoliers. One man who picked up his bandolier being hit in seven places, but not dangerously. Many horses were also injured, and several had to be destroyed. That night our men lent a proportion of their blankets to the Carabiniers.

On the 15th, marched into Greylingstad.

Captain Spencer and 21 N.C.O.s joined from England.

Captain Spencer had gone to hospital on July 19th, 1901, and had been invalided home.

Lieut.-Col. Smithson, D.S.O., resumed command of the Regiment.

Vet.-Lieut. Lake joined.

The Regiment remained at Greylingstad till June 5th, during which time it refitted from Standeston, and got remounts, bringing the strength of the Regiment at the front up to 527 N.C.O.s and Men, and 510 horses. A lot of musketry was performed, and shooting competitions between the different units of the column were carried out. The National Scouts, attached to the J.M.R.s, were expected to carry off the prizes for these events. However, the boasted superiority of the Dutchman as a marksman was not apparent on these occasions. We won the first, second, and third prizes for the Lloyd-Lindsay competition.

On May 17th, Colonel Allenby went down country on leave and Colonel Smithson, D.S.O., took over command of the column.

During the last week of May, the enemy, under Commandant Britz made a successful raid on the transport cattle at Standerton. Lieut.-Colonel Jenner took out all available men of General Bruce Hamilton's details, including 70 men of the 13th Hussars, under Captain Battye. The enemy made a stand on a kopje about seven miles south-east of Standerton, but were driven off by the Mounted Infantry, who suffered a few casualties. While retiring, the enemy lit a grass fire, which came on with great rapidity, and it was owing to the resource and initiation of No. 3919 Lce.-Corpl. Haslam that a wounded man of the Rifle Brigade was not caught in the fire. This N.C.O., with his section, galloped through the fire round the kopje, and though he was severely burnt himself, he brought back the wounded man, who lay helpless.

All this time the rumours indicated immediate and absolute surrender one day, and the next day it was just as confidently affirmed that all peace negociations were off, and that the columns were to move out again immediately. When about 8.30 a.m. on June 1st Lord Kitchener's telegram, announcing that peace had been declared, was given out, there was a scene of great enthusiasm throughout the camp.

At 12 o'clock the Regiment turned out, and gave three cheers (and a good many more, too) for the King, and thus, so far as we were concerned, ended the great Boer war of 1899—1902.

On the 2nd June, Capt. and Brevet-Major Tremayne and 10 N.C.O.s and men proceeded down country to represent the Regiment at the Coronation, and had a hearty send-off from their less fortunate comrades.

On the 5th, marched to Vlakfontein, where the Carabiniers left the Column, and joined McKenzie's Column.

Lieut. Hodgkinson, R.S.M. Daymond, and 39 N.C.O.s and men proceeded by rail to Pretoria to attend the thanksgiving service.

On the 6th, marched to Kraal.

The following telegram to Lord Kitchener from the Secretary of State for War was published for information :—

"His Majesty's Goverment offer to you their most sincere congratulations on the energy, skill, and patience with which you have conducted this prolonged campaign, and would wish you to communicate to the troops under your command their profound sense of the spirit, and endurance, with which they have met every call made upon them, of their bravery in action, of the excellent discipline preserved, of the humanity shown by them throughout ths trying period."

On the 7th, marched to Heidelberg, and remained there on the 8th. A thanksgivng service was held, which was attended by about 2,000 troops.

On the 9th, the 8th Hussars joined the column.

Marched to near Springs.

On the 10th, marched to Valkfontein.

On the 11th, marched to Irene.

On the 12th, marched to Pretoria.

On the 15th, the details left Standerton by rail for Pretoria, arriving there two days later.

On the 15th, the following extract from the "Gazette" dated 23rd May, 1902, was published:—

"13th Hussars.

"Lieut. John T. Wigan to be Captain in succession to Major E. A. Wiggin, who holds an extra-regimental appointment. Dated 26th March, 1902."

"The promotions to the ranks of Captain of the undermentioned Lieutenants are ante-dated as follows:

"F. G. Bayley to 24th February, in succession to Major C. Williams, who holds a staff appointment.

"A. W. B. Spencer to 24th February, 1902."

On the 24th, the column was broken up, and Colonel Allenby issued the folowing order:—

desires to express his thanks to all ranks of the Regiment for the good service they have rendered him during the time they have been with his column."

The day before Lord Kitchener left Pretoria for England he inspected the 8th and 13th Hussars, and thanked them for their services during the campaign. He said that he regretted that he was unable to personally see each cavalry regiment, but he hoped that all ranks would tell their comrades in other corps how much he appreciated the work the cavalry had performed.

On the 23rd, Special Army Order, dated 23rd April, 1902:—

"Before leaving South Africa the G.O.C. in Chief wishes to express his best thanks to all General Officers, Officers, N.C.O.s, and men, for the excellent service they have rendered since he first took over command, some 18 months ago. The period in question has offered few opportunities for those decisive engagements which keep up the spirit of an army, and add brilliance and interest in its operations. On the other hand, officers and men have been called upon for unceasing and ever increasing exertions, in face of great hardships and difficulties against a dangerous and elusive antagonist. The conduct of the troops under these trying circumstances has been beyond all praise.

"Never has there been the smallest sign of slackness or impatience, and it seems to Lord Kitchener that the qualities of endurance and resolution thus displayed are much more valuable to a commander than any dashing or short-lived effort by which some hard fought actions may be won in a campaign of ordinary duration.

"The G.O.C. in Chief has also special pleasure in congratulating the Army on the kindly and humane spirit by which all ranks have been animated during this long struggle. Fortunately for the future of South Africa the truth in this matter is known to our late enemy as well as to ourselves, and no misrepresentation from outside can prevail in the long run against the actual fact that no war has ever yet been waged in which combatants and non-combatants on either sides, have shewn so much consideration and kindness to one another.

"This message would be incomplete if reference were not made to the soldierly qualities displayed throughout the campaign by our quondam enemies, and to the admirable spirit displayed by them in carrying out the surrender of their arms.

"Many of the Boer leaders, who at an earlier date recognised the futility of carrying on a devastating conflict beyond a certain point, have already, for some time, served with us in the field and the help which they rendered us will not be forgotten. Many also of those who continued the struggle to the end have expressed a hope that on some future occasion they may have an opportunity of serving side by side with His Majesty's Forces from whom they will receive a very hearty welcome.

"In bidding the Army of South Africa farewell, it only remains for Lord Kitchener to wish every individual serving therein all happiness and prosperity for the future."

In Lord Kitchener's final despatch dated June 23rd, 1902, the names of the following Officers, N.C.O.'s, and Men were mentioned:—

"Lieut.-Colonel Smithson, D.S.O., Captains E. W. Denny, F. G. Bayley, Lieut. W. Pepys, S.S.M. J. F. Prentice, Sergt. W. H. Campbell, Lce.-Corpl. A. Levey, Pte. R. Blackley."

On the 24th, Major Williams rejoined the Regiment, from General Elliot's staff.

On the 30th, the following extracts from the "Gazette" were published for information:—

"War Office, June 3rd.

"13th Hussars.

"The promotion of 2nd Lieut. C. Elliot is antedated to February 24th. 2nd Lieut. R. B. Baggallay to be Lieutenant, vice Wigan promoted (March 26th).

"Lieut. H. Norfolk from 1st V.B. East Kent Regiment, to be 2nd Lieutenant (June 4th)."

Orders had been received on arrival in Pretoria to make the strength of horses up to 500. All sick and unsuitable horses were sent to the Sick Horse Depot, Remount Department, or Mounted Infantry, and others to complete the establishment were obtained from the Remount Department. The last of the horses required were received on July 3rd.

On the 5th, Lieut. J. D. Lyons, who had been invalided home from the effect of a wound received on November 8th, 1900, rejoined, with a draft of 48 N.C.O.s and men.

On July 8th, Captain Stern and 100 reservists and time-expired men sailed for England.

On the 14th, Major C. Williams proceeded down country on his way home.

On July 16th, Captain Church went down country on his way home, and was followed the next day by Lieuts. Hodgkinson, Marchant, and Jenkins.

On the 17th, Captain F. G. Bayley rejoined from General Burn-Murdoch's staff.

On the 21st, the stock-taking board was held, and thanks to Lieut. and Qrmr. Rupert, the Regiment was found to be in a very complete condition.

The following extract from the "Gazette" was published:—

"Brevet to be Lieut.-Col., Major Coventry Williams, 13th Hussars, dated 26th June, 1903."

On the 30th, Captain L. S. Battye and 83 reservists and time-expired men went down on their way home.

On the 18th August, Veterinary-Lieut. B. L. Lake left the Regiment to do duty with the 10th Hussars, being replaced by Civil Vet.-Surgeon Grist. 22 reservists and time-expired men left for England.

On the 20th, Civil-Surgeon A. G. Stewart sailed for England.

Civil-Surgeon R. G. Abercrombie was attached to the Regiment.

All horses were handed over to the 7th and 8th Hussars.

September 3rd, Major Ogilvy retired from the service, and Brevet-Major Tremayne was promoted to be Major.

On the 3rd, Lieut. Twist rejoined from the Cavalry Depot, Mooi River.

On the 6th, Captain A. H. Taylor, D.S.O., rejoined from General Burn-Murdoch's staff.

On the 10th, orders were received that the Regiment would leave Pretoria on the 12th, en route to East London, and would embark on the s.s. City of Vienna, sailing on the 17th.

On the 12th, the Regiment, after being inspected by General Lyttleton at the station, who wished us bon voyage, left Pretoria about 11 a.m., and arrived at East London during the evening of the 16th, and went into camp on the race course.

The City of Vienna did not arrive till the 19th, and the following day the Regiment embarked, which took some time, as it was a rough sea, and men and stores, etc., had to be taken out to the ship in tugs.

Lieut.-Colonel Smithson, D.S.O., took over command of the troops on board, and Captain Taylor, D.S.O., assumed command of the Regiment.

The City of Vienna sailed for Capetown on the 21st, and had a very rough passage, so rough that though she arrived outside the harbour on the 24th, she was not able to go in till the following day.

The officers that sailed on this ship were:—
  Lieut.-Colonel Smithson, D.S.O.
  Captain A. H. Taylor, D.S.O.
  Captain and Adjt. E. W. Denny.
  Captain F. G. Bayley.
  Captain A. W. B. Spencer.
  Captain J. T. Wigan.
  Lieut. J. D. Lyons.
  Lieut. E. F. Twist.
  Lieut. L. B. B Gubbins.
  Lieut. W. F. V. Cosens.

Lieut. A. W. Kennard.
Lieut. C. Elliot.
Lieut. R. B. B. Baggallay.
Lieut. and Qrmr. G. Rupert, 1 Warrant Officer.
539 N.C.O.s, and Men.

The other troops on board were the 5th Lancers, a detachment of the R.A.M.C., and details from various units.

On October 12th, arrived at S. Vincent and coaled, and arrived at Southampton on the night of the 20th. The Regiment disembarked the following morning, three years all but three weeks since it had left England, being welcomed home by General Sir Baker Russell, and many other old officers of the Regiment, and entrained for Aldershot, to be quartered in the East Cavalry Barracks.

Among the special promotions which appeared in the "Gazette" in October, were the following:—

"To be Brevet Lieut.-Colonels, Major C. Williams (June 26th); Major E. A. Wiggin (August 22nd).

"To be Brevet Mapor, Captain E. W. Denny, August 22nd).

To have honorary rank of Captain, Qrmr. and Hon. Lieut. G. Rupert (August 22nd)."

Extract from 1st Army Corps Orders, dated 15th September, 1902:—

"The following resolution of the House of Lords and the House of Commons is published for information:—

"House of Lords and Commons,
"Die Jovis, 5th Junij, 1902.

"Resolved, Nemine Dissentiente, by the Lords Spiritual, and Temporal in Parliament assembled.

"That the thanks of this House be given to the Officers of the Army for the energy and gallantry with which they executed the services which they were called upon to perform during the prolonged campaign in South Africa.

"Resolved, Nemine Dissentiente. That this House doth acknowledge, and highly approve, the gallantry, discipline, and good conduct displayed by the N.C.O.s and Men of the Army throughout the war.

"That this House doth acknowledge, with admiration, the distinguished valour, devotion, and conduct of those officers and men who have perished during the campaign in South Africa, in the service of the Empire, and desire to express deep sympathy with their relatives and friends."

DEATHS IN SOUTH AFRICA.

3733 Private Billington, 16th Dec., 1899; drowned, Chieveley.

3016 Private Ross, 20th Dec., 1899; killed in action, Chieveley.

4051 Private Smith, 20th Dec., 1899; killed in action, Chieveley.

2862 Private Giuler, 17th Jan., 1900; drowned, Trichaard's Drift.

3767 Private Wright, 5th Feb., 1900; dysentry, Mooi River.

3792 Private Russell, 28th Feb., 1900; enteric, Pietermaritzberg.

3939 Lce.-Cpl. Watt, 7th March, 1900; killed in action, Sunday River.

3011 Private Fletcher, 19th March, 1900; enteric, Sunday River.

4313 Private Vincent, 16th March, 1900; enteric, Ladysmith.

3819 Private Gilham, 24th March, 1900; enteric, Chieveley.

3669 Private Miles, 21st March, 1900; enteric, Sunday River.

3246 Private Shailor, 31st March, 1900; enteric, Sunday River.

3396 Private Ramsden, 3rd April, 1900; enteric, Sunday River.

3872 Private Whatman, 2nd April, 1900; dysentry, Sunday River.

SOUTH AFRICAN WAR.

3838 Private Heath, 16th April, 1900; enteric, Sunday River.
3434 Private Bull, 23rd April, 1900; enteric, Ladysmith.
4136 Private Coomber, 23rd April, 1900; dysentry, Ladysmith.
3407 Private Smith, 22nd April, 1900; pneumonia, Ladysmith.
3982 Private Glenny, 24th April, 1900: enteric, Ladysmith.
3077 Private Hunter, 4th May, 1900; enteric, Ladysmith.
3666 Private Roche, 4th May, 1900; enteric, Modder Spruit.
4147 Private Gibbs, 10th May, 1900; enteric, Ladysmith.
3411 Private Brennan, 16th May, 1900; enteric, Ladysmith.
4066 Private Venn, 19th May, 1900; enteric, Ladysmith.
3214 Private Morris, 14th May, 1900; wounds, Newcastle.
4612 Lc.-Cpl. Barber, 24th May, 1900; enteric, Ladysmith.
3829 Private Lipscombe, 24th May, 1900; enteric, Ladysmith.
4617 Private Chandler, 24th May, 1900; enteric, Ladysmith.
3832 Private Read, 28th May, 1900; enteric, Ladysmith.
3885 Private Prodger, 2nd June, 1900; enteric, Ladysmith.
3295 Private Wooder, 2nd June, 1900; enteric, Daunhauser.

13th HUSSARS.

3306 Private Kent, 6th June, 1900; enteric, Ladysmith.

4835 Private Waugh, 14th June, 1900, dysentry, Ladysmith.

4615 Private Brown, 17th June, 1900; enteric, Estcourt.

4817 Private Hines, 23rd June, 1900; enteric, Ladysmith.

3285 Private Wilson, 30th June, 1900; dysentry, Capetown.

3711 Private Matthews, 6th July, 1900; enteric, Ladysmith.

3993 Corporal Roache, 10th July, 1900; enteric, Standerton.

4168 Private Lewis, 7th August, 1900; enteric, Ladysmith.

4020 Private Dempsey, 22nd August, 1900; killed in action, Newcastle.

4866 Private Mitchell, 3rd Sept., 1900; pneumonia, Standerton.

2749 S.S.M. Lightfoot, 27th Nov., 1900; aneurism, Pietermaritzberg.

4840 Private Melton, 31st December, 1900; dysentry, Standerton.

3740 Private Petherham, 1st Jan., 1901; enteric, Standerton.

3208 Private Walsh, 13th Jan., 1901; enteric, Standerton.

3703 Private Brown, 16th Jan., 1901; enteric, Standerton.

5450 Private Langdon, 28th Jan., 1901; enteric, Standerton.

3533 Private Watts, 31st Jan., 1901; enteric, Heidelberg.

SOUTH AFRICAN WAR.

- 4227 Private Hill, 4th Feb., 1901; enteric, Heidelberg.
- 3267 Private Heaps, 23rd Feb., 1901; wounds, Standerton.
- 3776 Sergeant Mahon, 15th March, 1901; wounds, De Lange's Drift.
- 4773 Private Bakewell, 29th April, 1901; killed in action, Greylingstad.
- 4281 Private Hayes, 29th April, 1901; killed in action, Uitkyk.
- 4290 Private Mills, 29th April, 1901; killed in action, Uitkyk.
- 3791 Private Holland, 29th April, 1901; killed in action, Uitkyk.
- 3880 Private Basden, 29th April, 1901; killed in action, Uitkyk.
- 4955 Private Hessey, 20th May, 1901; enteric, Standerton.
- 4280 Private Trow, 26th May, 1901; enteric, Heidelberg.
- 4942 Private Smith, 30th May, 1901; drowned: De Pan-lower Waterval.
- 5464 Private Platford, 9th June, 1901; enteric, Standerton.
- 2711 Private Smith, 7th Sept., 1901; killed in action, Klerksdorp.
- 3981 Private Mackie, 7th Sept., 1901; killed in action, Klerksdorp.
- 3592 Private Tanner, 8th Sept., 1901; killed in action, Klerksdorp.
- 5146 Private Smith, 4th Oct., 1901; enteric, Mooi River.
- 4096 Private Hutchins, 11th Oct., 1901; enteric, Dundee.

13th HUSSARS.

4801 Private Woodward, 23rd Sept., 1901; erysipelas, Klerksdorp.
5193 Private Prior, 17th Oct., 1901; enteric, Johannesberg.
3050 Corporal Campbell (att. S.A.L.H.), 26th Oct., 1901; died of wounds, Witbank, O.R.C.
3963 Private White, 1st Nov., 1901; died of wounds, Trichaardsfontein.
5136 Private Dell, 4th Nov., 1901; enteric, Utrecht.
5139 Private Brown, 5th Nov., 1901; enteric, Elandsfontein.
5811 Private Brown, 15th Nov., 1901; enteric, Pretoria.
4385 Private Culle— 5th Feb., 1902; enteric, Ermelo.
4590 Private Edwards, 18th Feb., 1902; enteric, Standerton.
5029 Private Calton, 27th Feb., 1902; enteric, Elandsfontein.
4587 Private Johnston, 5th March, 1902; dysentry, Ermelo.
5315 Private Wright, 18th March, 1902; pneumonia, Charlestown.
4496 Private House, 14th July, 1902; enteric, Heilbron.
2685 Sergeant Hoare, 15th Oct., 1902; hemiplegia, Wynburg. (
3815 Private Francis (transferred to S.A.C.); no information.

```
Killed and died of wounds ............... 17
Enteric ..................................... 46
Dysentry .................... .................. 7
Drowned ................. ...................... 3
Pneumonia ............. ..................... 3
Aneurism ............... ...................... 1
Erysipelas .................................... 1
Hemiplegia ......... ......................... 1
No information .............................. 1
                                              ——
                                              80
```

WOUNDED.

Lieut. J. T. Wigan, 7th March, 1900, Sunday River.
Major K. McLaren, 31st March, 1900, near Mafeking.
Major W. C. Smithson, 22nd August, Newcastle.
Lieut. J. D. Lyons, 8th Sept., 1900, Eden Kop.
3133 Private Humphry, 15th December, 1899, Colenso.
3767 Private Wright, 15th Dec., 1899, Colenso.
3654 Lc.-Cpl. Coghlan, 19th Jan., 1900, Spion Kop.
4126 Pte. Findley, 19th Jan., 1900, Spion Kop.
2998 Private Judge, 25th Jan., 1900, Spion Kop.
3652 Private Rugg, 7th March, 1900, Sunday River.
3214 Private Morris, 5th April, 1900, Wessels Nek (died 14th May, 1900).
4624 Private Gilchrist, 21st August, 1900, Newcastle.
4843 Private Willis, 21st August, 1900, Newcastle.
3831 Lc.-Corpl. Cooke, 22nd Aug., 1900, Newcastle.
4191 Private Trustram, 9th Sept., Umbana.
3671 Private Broderick, 20th Sept., 1900, Rademeyer's Farm.
4083 Private Lewis, 29th Sept., 1900, near Platrand.
3400 Private Elsegood, 19th Oct., 1900, Waterval.
4107 Private Ware, 2nd Dec., 1900, near Standerton.
4063 Lc.-Cpl. Bradley, 17th Dec., 1900, near Vlakfontein.
3181 Private McMasters, 19th Dec., 1900, near Vlakfontein.
4948 Private Lee, 19th Dec., 1900, Frischgevaad.

4142 Private Brewer, 15th Jan., 1901, near Reitvlei, north-east of Standerton.
4887 Pte. Mitchell, 15th Jan., 1901, near Reitvlei, north-east of Standerton.
3051 Pte. Pollock, 16th Jan., 1901, near Reitvlei, north east of Standerton.
3518 Private Sutton, 16th Jan., 1901, near Reitvlei, north-east of Standerton.
4820 Private Parr, 15th March, 1900, De Lange's Drift.
4861 Private McSweeney, 15th March,1901,De Lange's Drift.
4846 Private Letts, 26th March, 1901, Rietspruit.
3548 Corporal Gavin, 23rd March, 1901, Vogelstruisfontein.
3781 Lc.-Cpl. Hedley, 11th April, 1901, Nigel Mines.
4409 Private Prince, 29th April, 1901, Greylingstad.
4404 Lc.-Cpl. Capper, 29th April, 1901, Greylingstad.
4296 Lc.-Cpl. House, 29th April, 1901, Uitkyk.
4183 Private Hawkins, 20th May, 1901, De Lange's Drift.
3898 Pte. Hanton, 22nd May, 1901, De Lange's Drift.
4043 Private Weale, 31st May, 1901, Weilfontein.
4618 Private Dewhurst, 31st May, 1901, Weilfontein.
3734 Lc.-Cpl. Harding, 31st May, 1901, Weilfontein.
4065 Private Garrett, 22nd July, 1901, Klipfontein.
4018 Private Frane, 23rd July, 1901, Woolmaranstad.
4586 Private Adams, 23rd July, 1901, Woolmaranstad.
2408 Private Pritchard, 25th August, 1901, Oliphant's Nek.
4821 Pte. Mallard, 7th Sept. 1901, Klerksdorp.
3531 Sergeant Lloyd, 1st Nov., 1901, Trichaardsfontein.
4836 Corporal Mumford, 1st Nov., 1901, Trichaardsfontein.

SOUTH AFRICAN WAR.

4368 Private Musgrave, 1st Nov., 1901, Trichaardsfontein.

3550 Private Cleaver, 5th Jan., 1902, Bultfontein.

3563 Sergeant Hetherington, 5th Jan., 1902, Bultfontein.

3554 Lc.-Cpl. Dennis, 15th March, 1902, Broedersrust

The total number of N.C.O.s and Men on the strength of the Regiment in South Africa was 1,376.

The total number of men invalided home was 296. Many of these came out a second time.

150 of the N.C.O.s and Men who left England with the Regiment returned with it, without having been home.

HONOURS.

Colonel H. J. Blagrove.................. C.B.
Major W. C. Smithson .... D.S.O.
Captain K. McLaren .... D.S.O.
Captain A. H. R. Ogilvy .... D.S.O.
Captain A. H. M. Taylor .... D.S.O.
Sergt. W. Mahon (since deceased) D.C.M.
Private S. Herbert .... D.C.M.
Private E. Servey .... D.C.M.
S.S.M. J. F. Prentice............... D.C.M.
Lce.-Corpl. A. Levey .... D.C.M.

BREVETS.

Major C. Williams .... Brevet Lieut.-Col. June 26th, 1902.

Capt. E. A. Wigan .... Brevet Major, November 29th, 1900.
Brevet Lieut.-Col. August 22nd, 1902.

Capt. J. H. Tremayne .... Brevet Major 29th January, 1902.

Capt. E. W. Denny .... Brevet Major August 22nd, 1902.

Qrmr. and Hon. Lieut. G. Rupert to have the Hon. rank of Captain, August 22nd.

SOUTH AFRICAN WAR.

MENTIONED IN DESPATCHES.

Lieut.-Col. Smithson.
Lieut.-Col. Williams.
Major K. McLaren.
Lieut.-Col. E. A. Wiggin.
Major J. H. Tremayne.
Captain A. H. M. Taylor.
Captain J. F. Church.
Captain A. Symons.
Captain and Brevet-Major E. W. Denny.
Captain F. G. Bayley.
Lieut. W. Pepys.
2nd Lieut. C. C. Dangar.
Corporal F. Smith.
Private A. Cook.
Private J. Pritchard.
Private S. Herbert.
Lce.-Corporal J. T. Harding.
Private T. Dempster.
Private R. Tanner (since deceased).
Corporal W. H. Campbell, att S.A.L.H.
Pte. E. Servey.
S.S.M. J. F. Prentice.
Private T. Farrance.
Sergt. W. Mahon (since deceased).
Private R. Blackley.
S.S.M. E. Doran (with 8th Batt. I.Y.)
S.S.M. F. G. Brown.

RESERVE SQUADRON.

On the Regiment leaving Aldershot in November, 1899, the Reserve Squadron was just under 400 strong.

Captain A. H. Ogilvy commanded the squadron, and had with him 2nd Lieut. G. H. Hodgkinson, and Lieut. and Riding-Master R. McWalter, who took up the duties of Adjutant and Quarter-Master.

A few days after the Regiment sailed 2nd Lieut. L. B. B. Gubbins joined, and on November 15th 2nd Lieut. Lambert was gazetted.

On November 21st, the Reserve Squadron moved to Hounslow, leaving at Aldershot about 200 mobilized reservists.

On November 20th, 2nd Lieut. W. F. U. Cosens was gazetted to the Regiment.

On December 1st, a draft of 50 Reservists left to join the 19th Hussars.

On December 9th, 2nd Lieuts. C. E. Jenkins and G. Halswelle were gazetted to the Regiment.

At the end of 1899, the strength of this squadron was eight Officers, one Warrant Officer, 478 N.C.O.s and Men, and 124 horses.

79 19th Hussars reservists were also attached.

SOUTH AFRICAN WAR.

While at Hounslow the Reserve Squadron acted as a receiving depot to forward horses to South Africa.

Between January and May, 626 horses passed through their hands.

On January 31st, 2nd Lieut. G. H. Hodgkinson sailed for South Africa in charge of a draft for the Regiment.

In January, Captain E. A. Critchley, Reserve of Officers (4th Hussars). joined for duty; Hon. Major A. Leetham, Reserve of Officers (13th Hussars), joined in February, and Licut, and Riding-Master Percy, 19th Hussars, and Lieut. F. N. Q. Shaldham, late 13th Hussars, joined in March.

On March 21st, 2nd Lieut. Kennard was gazetted, and on April 21st, 2nd Lieut. C. Elliot was gazetted.

On April 5th, Major-General Sir Henry Trotter, K.C.V.O., Commanding the Home District, inspected the squadron.

Between Janaury and May, drafts amounting to 1,539 N.C.O.s and Men were sent out to South Africa, India, and to Canterbury.

The strength of the Squadron on May 31st was 723 N.C.O.s and Men.

On May 10th, the Squadron proceeded to Norwich.

On May 19th, 2nd Lieuts. Gubbins and Lambert sailed with a draft for the Regiment and on June 2nd, 2nd Lieuts. Cosens and Jenkins sailed with a draft.

On July 14th, Hon. Major Leetham resumed duty with the Monmouthshire Militia Engineers, and was struck off the strength of the squadron.

On July 17th, Major J. F. Murphy, Lieuts. A. W. B. Spencer and J. T. Wigan, who had been invalided home from South Africa, joined for duty.

Majorf Murphy took over command of the squadron, and Captain Ogilvy proceeded to South Africa to join the Regiment.

On July 22nd, the Regiment furnished the escort to H.R.H. the Prince of Wales on the occasion of his opening the Jenny Lind Hospital at Norwich. 2nd Lieut. G. Halswelle commanded the escort.

Major General Sir W. F. Gatacre, K.C.B., notified in District Orders His Royal Highness' entire satisfaction at the way the escort was turned out, and performed their duties.

In July. Major-General H. F. Grant, C.B., Inspector General of Cavalry, inspected the squadron, and complimented Captain Ogilvy on the system of training that he had instituted.

On July 30th, Lieut. Friar, 4th Hussars, joined for duty.

On August 9th, Major General Sir W. F. Gatacre K.C.B., Commanding the Eastern District, inspected pleased with what he saw. The squadron paraded 1,030 strong.

In August, Captain T. B. Phillips, Reserve of Officers (13th Hussars), joined for duty.

2nd Lieut. R. B. Baggallay was gazetted on September 19th.

Between May and the end of the year, 804 men, and 231 horses were sent out to South Africa, and India.

At the end of the year the strength of the squadron was eight Officers, one Warrant Officer, 727 N.C.O.s and Men, and 189 horses.

On January 22nd, 1901, Her Most Gracious Majesty the Queen died, and at her funeral the Regiment was represented by a mounted squadron, 80 strong, under Major Murphy, and a dismounted party, 150 strong, under Lieut. F. N. Q. Shuldham. Lieut. and Riding-Master R. McWalter was in charge of the baggage of all mounted troops from the Eastern District that proceeded to London for this ceremony.

On 2nd March, Lieut. Wigan, 2nd Lieuts. Lambert, Halswelle, Kennard, and Elliot, sailed for South Africa with a draft of 305 N.C.O.s and Men.

On 17th April, 1901, the Reserve Squadron, under Captain T. B. Phillips, proceeded to Hounslow to be incorporated with the 2nd Provisonal Regiment of Hussars, commanded by Lieut.-Colonel F. Butler, Reserve of Officers, 4th Hussars.

Major Murphy and Lieut. and Riding-Master McWalter, with the band, remained at Norwich till August 23rd, when they joined the 2nd Provisional Regiment of Hussars at Hounslow.

On the Reserve Squadron joining the 2nd Provisional Regiment of Hussars, it was split up into three squadrons, as follows:—

13TH HUSSARS.

    B Squadron, under Captain T. B. Phillips.
    D Squadron, under Major F. J. Murphy.
    E Squadron, under Lieut. and Riding Master R. McWalter.

The remainder of this Provisional Regimnet was composed of 10th Royal Hussars.

On the Reserve Squadron joining the 2nd Provisional Regiment of Hussars, all the equipment, clothing, and other accounts of the squadron were closed, shewing a deficit of £4 17s., which was written off by the sanction of the G.O.C., Home District, as being under £10. This was mainly due to the careful and systematic manner in which Lieut. and Riding-Master McWalter had performed the duties of acting-quartermaster.

On March 26th, 1902, Major Murphy retired from the Service. The Reserve Squadron left Hounslow on September 18th, 1902, and proceeded to Aldershot, and took over the East Cavalry Baracks.(

The strength of the squadron on arrival at Aldershot was 857 N.C.O.s and Men, and 185 horses.

The Regiment arrived at Aldershot on October 21st, 1902.

MAY & CO., PRINTERS, WELLINGTON STREET, ALDERSHOT.

www.ingramcontent.com/pod-product-compliance
Lightning Source LLC
Chambersburg PA
CBHW072128160426
43197CB00012B/2031